THE BEST OF
NATIONAL GEOGRAPHIC

YEARBOOK 2013

Red-hot lava from Pu'u 'O'o in
Hawai'i Volcanoes National Park
streams over a moon-like landscape
carved from almost 30 years of
continuous lava flow.

THE BEST OF
NATIONAL GEOGRAPHIC

YEARBOOK 2013

NATIONAL GEOGRAPHIC

WASHINGTON, D.C.

These BASE jumpers on Half Dome in Yosemite National Park, California, take the easy way down by parachuting into the valley. Part of the risk in jumping from this spot comes from the fact that it is an illegal activity.

CONTENTS

Covered in pollen and looking like it is sporting the latest sunglass trend, a curious fly examines the camera.

A Year with National Geographic

Welcome to the first ever National Geographic *Yearbook* for 2013! We are thrilled to be bringing you the best National Geographic has to offer—from the most amazing photographs to the latest advancements in science, space, technology and natural history.

Join us for a tour of the world, from Antarctica's newly discovered 'albino' penguin to the farthest reaches of the moon's molten core. From cover to cover, we've packed this volume with world-class photographs that will amaze and amuse (see page 63 for elephants as you've never seen them before) and reveal stories you will barely believe (did you know that piranhas talk to each other or that women can sniff out men? Both true). And, of course, National Geographic researchers and explorers around the world have verified these amazing facts, so we are delivering the very best to you and your family.

With *The Best of National Geographic: Yearbook 2013*, we hope that you also will enjoy the chance to become a bit of a National Geographic explorer in your own backyard. Every month, you'll discover which constellation to look for and how to identify them in the night sky. You can also test your global geographic knowledge (where are the ruins of Persepolis? Answer page 154). And for some brain-teasing fun, challenge yourself to a bit of Sudoku (go on, give them a try!). And enjoy loads more photographs and mind-expanding trivia.

National Geographic is committed to bringing you the best, all year round. Happy discoveries—and best wishes for 2013!

—Anne Alexander
Editorial Director, National Geographic Books

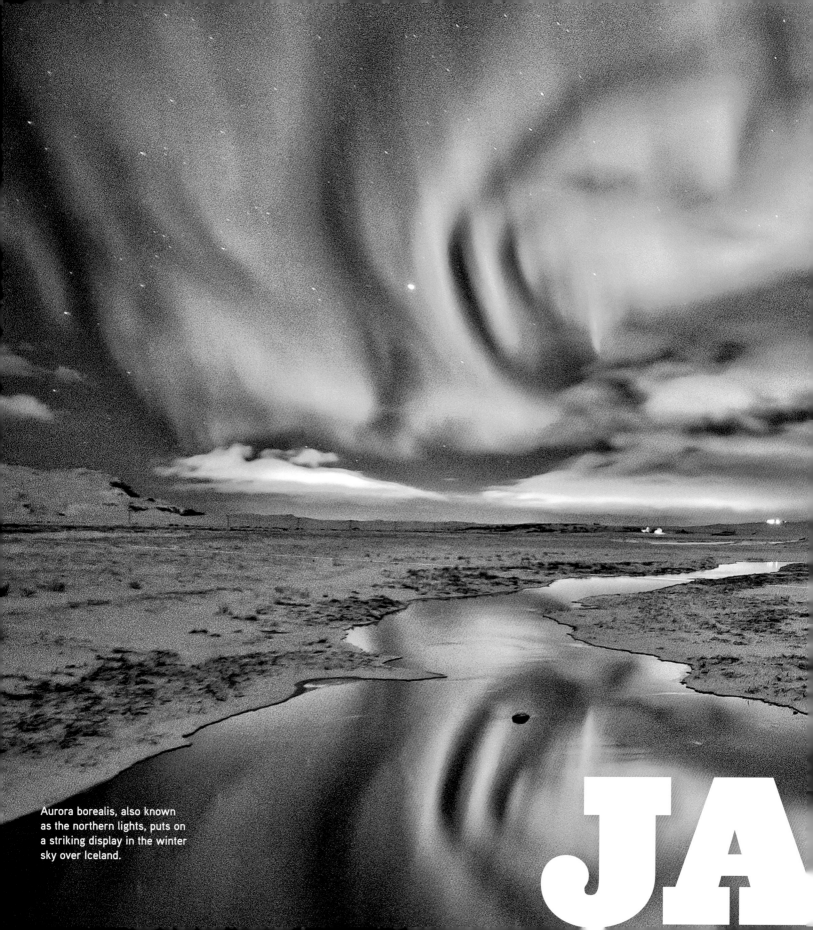

Aurora borealis, also known as the northern lights, puts on a striking display in the winter sky over Iceland.

JA

COME, YE COLD WINDS, AT JANUARY'S CALL

NUARY

1 TUESDAY — New Year's Day

2 WEDNESDAY — Hogmanay Bank Holiday (Scotland)

3 THURSDAY

4 FRIDAY ◑

5 SATURDAY

6 SUNDAY

7 MONDAY

8 TUESDAY

9 WEDNESDAY

10 THURSDAY

11 FRIDAY ●

12 SATURDAY

13 SUNDAY — National Geographic's 125th anniversary

14 MONDAY

15 TUESDAY

16 WEDNESDAY

17 THURSDAY

18 FRIDAY ◑

19 SATURDAY

20 SUNDAY

21 MONDAY

22 TUESDAY

23 WEDNESDAY

24 THURSDAY

25 FRIDAY — Burns Night (Scotland)

26 SATURDAY ○

27 SUNDAY

28 MONDAY

29 TUESDAY

30 WEDNESDAY

31 THURSDAY

Bird of the Month

Smew *(Mergellus albellus)*

LENGTH: 38–44 cm
RANGE: Northern Europe and northern Asia

Smew is most likely a corrupted version of the Middle English semawe, 'sea mew'. Mergus comes from the Latin merger 'to dive' and albellus meaning 'whitish' comes from the Latin albus and refers to the bird's colouring.

GEO PUZZLE

Sudoku Challenge

1		9	5		7	8		4
	4						6	
3		7				1		5
			8	7	9			
	7						2	
			1	6	2			
7		1				4		8
	3						1	
6		2	4		1	3		9

Answers on p. 156

A painting by artist Stanley Meltzoff depicts the original gathering of the National Geographic Society's founders at Washington's Cosmos Club in January 1888.

THE BEGINNING OF NATIONAL GEOGRAPHIC

The National Geographic Society has reported on 'the world and all that is in it' for 125 years. The seed for this global audience was planted in Washington, D.C., on 13 January 1888. A group of 33 of the city's scientific and intellectual leaders met at the famed Cosmos Club to consider 'the advisability of organising a society for the increase and diffusion of geographical knowledge'. They were passionate young men with widely ranging professions from geologists to cartographers to bankers to military men. Among their ranks was John Wesley Powell, famous for his pioneering exploration of the Grand Canyon, and Adolphus W. Greely, chief signal officer of the U.S. Army and noted polar explorer. ■

The cover of the first edition of *National Geographic* magazine from October 1888.

January Constellation

Betelgeuse sits on Orion's left shoulder and Rigel forms the right foot. At the sword you'll find the Orion Nebula. Just to the northwest of Betelgeuse is Taurus and the two famed star clusters, the Pleiades and the Hyades. To the northeast of Orion, Gemini is marked by the stars Castor and Pollux.

ORION

MAKEUP: 20 stars
BEST VIEWED: Jan/Feb
LOCATION: Winter, southeast quadrant
SIZE IN THE SKY: ✋
ALPHA STAR: Betelgeuse
DEEP SKY OBJECT: Orion Nebula

Mythology There are a few stories in Greco-Roman mythology associated with Orion. In one, Orion was a powerful hunter dealt a lethal sting by Scorpius—a reason for the two being placed on opposite sides of the sky.

In another story, Artemis, the goddess of the hunt, admired Orion for his great skill as a hunter. Her twin brother, Apollo, grew jealous. He tricked her into shooting Orion with a deadly arrow. Upon discovering what she had done, Artemis immortalised Orion in the stars.

About This may be the most recognisable constellation in the sky, visible worldwide and identified by many cultures. To modern sky watchers, the hunter's position is ideal for use as a reference point: Three of the twenty-five brightest stars in the sky are found in this group, and their brightness makes the structure of a man in the constellation easy to imagine. ▪

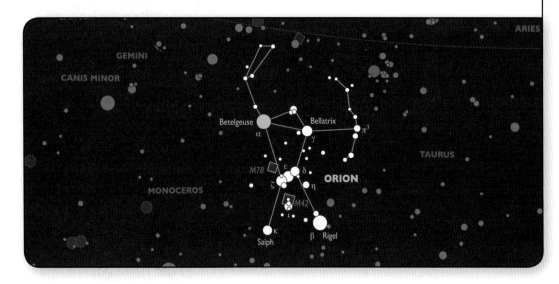

Ancient Bloom

A tiny five-centimetre fossil found in southern Argentina could offer clues to how sunflowers and daisies came to be so ubiquitous. At 47.5 million years old, it's the oldest evidence of the huge *Asteraceae* family—to which daisies belong—and supports the theory that the group first took root in South America.

One for the Record Books

A female polar bear swam for a record-breaking nine days straight, traversing 426 miles (687 kilometres) of water—roughly the distance between Glasgow and Southampton. The predator made her epic journey in the Beaufort Sea, where sea ice is shrinking due to global warming.

Global warming is forcing mother bears to swim greater and greater distances to reach land, to the peril of their cubs. The cub of the record-setting bear, for instance, died at some point between starting the swim and when the researchers next observed the mother on land. She also lost 22 per cent of her body weight. 'We're pretty sure that these animals didn't have to do these long swims before, because 426-mile stretches of open water didn't occur very often in the evolutionary history of the polar bear,' said study co-author Steven Amstrup, chief scientist for the conservation group Polar Bears International.

In 2010, Arctic sea ice extent

Polar bears are known to swim between land and sea ice floes to find hunting grounds. However, the shrinking of sea ice in the Arctic is forcing them to swim greater distances.

was the third lowest on record, part of a long-term trend of ice loss that will continue for decades to come, according to the National Snow and Ice Data Center in Boulder, Colorado. 'So the sort of conditions that contribute to long-distance swimming are likely going to persist in the future, and if cub mortality is directly related to this, then it would have a negative impact on the population,' said George Durner, a USGS research zoologist in Anchorage, Alaska. It's unknown whether the cubs are drowning at sea or whether the metabolically costly act of swimming long distances in nearly freezing water kills them after they reach land. ■

STRANGE . . . BUT TRUE!

The longest recorded flight of a chicken is 13 seconds.

Geography Q&A

Q **1** The Gulf of Riga is part of which European sea?

Q **2** Name the mountain range that stretches from the Bay of Biscay to the Mediterranean Sea.

Q **3** What country that borders Guatemala has English as its official language?

Answers on p. 154

A Better Brain Map

We brag about our grey matter, linking intelligence to brain cells. But for neuroscientists, it's about white matter and the networks that carry information between regions of the brain. Research teams are using cutting-edge scanners to create a library of 'connectomes'—maps of the brain's circuitry that promise to reveal how the organ responds to aging, learning and other events. Data from this project may provide insights into treating autism and schizophrenia. In a test image (above) is a colour-coded depiction of routes created by a brain's neural pathways. The picture's creator, Harvard professor Van Wedeen, has devised a 3-D imaging process that unveils the connections by tracing the movement of water along fibre tissues. ■

This colourful representation of the human brain is known as a diffusion spectrum image, and shows the connections that make up the brain's circuitry.

Red Alert!

A brilliant red dye derived from tiny insects once treasured by the Spanish conquistadores gives some modern foods and cosmetics an alluring blush. In a small number of people, though, it can cause swelling, rashes or respiratory problems. Under EU food directives, any product containing the colouring must now be labelled as containing carmine, the name given to the cochineal pigment.

Native to the New World, cactus-eating cochineal insects are dried and crushed to produce a powdered dye. Beginning in the 16th century, Europeans of wealth and status wore clothing reddened with rare cochineal. The deep, durable colour was even used to produce the British Army's famous red coats for more than 200 years. Cochineal harvesting declined after the invention of cheap synthetic dyes in the 1800s, but it has rebounded—mostly in Peru and the Canary Islands—with the dye's use as a natural alternative to artificial colourings. ■

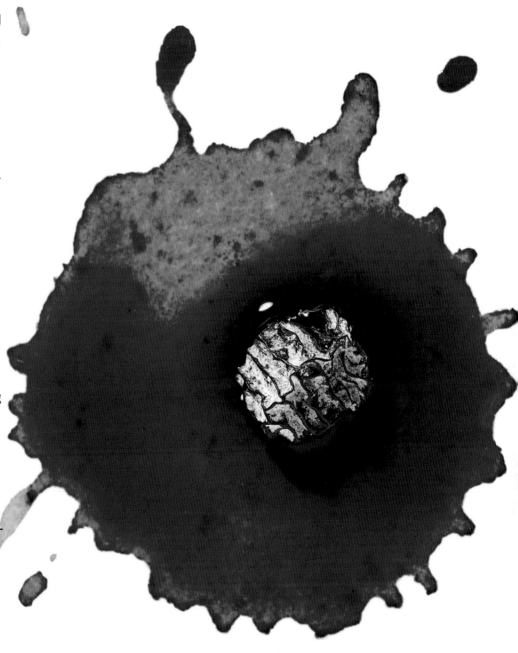

You may not realise it, but some of the food you eat could contain insects! Tiny bugs are crushed to make this red dye, used to colour confectionery as well as fabric and even makeup.

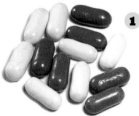

1 FOOD AND DRINK
Sweets, biscuits, yoghurts, gelatins and juices may contain cochineal, but enhanced reds in foodstuffs can also come from a synthetic colour.

2 TEXTILES
Embroidery thread, fabric for art and couture gowns are still hand-coloured with cochineal. Industrial dyers tend to use cheaper synthetics.

3 COSMETICS
Anything red, pink or brown in the makeup aisle—lipstick, blusher, mascara, eye liner, eye shadow, nail polish—may contain cochineal.

Sniffing Out the Opposite Sex

Humans can sniff out the opposite sex via odourless pheromones, a new study suggests. The discovery adds weight to the evidence that humans, much like the rest of the animal kingdom, know more from their noses than previously thought.

We know that for animals, chemosignals are actually the most used signals to communicate, whereas with humans, we think chemosensation is not really used,' said study leader Wen Zhou, a psychologist at the Chinese Academy of Sciences in Beijing. 'But based on our experiences, they are still influenced by these cues, even if they don't explicitly know it.'

In a recent experiment, subjects who smelled possible pheromones from the opposite sex were more likely to interpret ambiguous human figures as that sex, even when the participants didn't know they were smelling anything. Pheromones—chemicals that can communicate sexual information—are widespread in the animal world, and some research suggests humans use them unconsciously as well.

Zhou and colleagues used videos of points of light moving in a way that fools the eye into seeing human motion.

Men and women give out pheromones distinct to their sex. We know these chemical signals are important to animals, but until recently it was thought that humans didn't use them.

The videos were made by filming real people in motion-capture suits with LEDs at each joint—similar to the suits used to create Hollywood special effects. Scientists mathematically manipulated the dots until the 'figures' had neither a typically male nor typically female gait.

Twenty men and twenty women watched the video animations of these ambiguous figures, as well as ones that were more obviously male or female. While watching the videos, the subjects sniffed clove oil infused with the male steroid androstadienone, the female steroid estratetraenol or a plain oil used as a base for many cosmetics. Men who smelled the female pheromone were more likely to identify the androgynous walker as a woman. They were even likelier to identify more clearly male figures as female than those who just smelled clove oil. The same results applied when women sniffed the male compound.

This perception difference seems to be completely unrelated to what their noses told them; a blindfolded test subject couldn't tell the difference between steroid-infused clove oil and plain oil. 'It's completely below their awareness,' Zhou said. 'They didn't know what they were smelling, but their behaviour showed these different patterns.' ■

When looking for the perfect partner your nose is more important than you might think. Research suggests that we have the ability to tell someone's sex from the pheromones they give out.

New Year's Eve

Celebrations to welcome in the New Year have been around for over 4,000 years. For the Phoenicians and Persians, the year began with the autumnal equinox; for the Greeks it began with the winter solstice. Rites and ceremonies were held for both purgation of the old year and to express joy in life's renewal. Today, celebrations have grown to include New Year's Day. All kinds of traditions have sprung up around this symbolic fresh start, from songs ('Auld Lang Syne' from a Scottish poem) to foods (black-eyed peas for luck). Many think of New Year's Day as a time for connection and reflection—it's traditional to kiss your dearest at midnight. ■

Herb of the Month

Elder

TRADITIONAL USES:
Colds and flu

History Many centuries ago, conflicting superstitions surrounded elder. In some places, people thought that cutting down elder trees could anger supernatural beings who dwelled within them. Particularly frightening was the Elder Tree Mother, who sought revenge by haunting houses made of elder wood and harming infants lying in elder wood cradles. Elsewhere, elder was a symbol of protection. Planting elder near a house or nailing elder branches above the windows and doors kept witches at bay. Superstitions aside, elderberries are rich in vitamin C and antioxidants. Herbal practitioners recommend elderberry to fight infection and shorten a cold's duration. They suggest teas made from elder flowers for easing symptoms of colds, flu and bronchitis. ■

Strange . . . but True: Mammals

❶ A camel doesn't sweat until its body temperature reaches 41°C.

❷ Horses run on their toes.

❸ Bats are the only mammals that fly.

❹ The eastern spotted skunk does a handstand before it sprays.

❺ A grizzly bear can run as fast as a horse.

❻ A zedonk is a cross between a female donkey and a male zebra.

❼ A sloth would take a month to travel a single mile.

❽ Kangaroos don't hop backwards.

❾ Hippos can be more dangerous than lions.

❿ Blue whales are the largest animals that have ever lived—they're even bigger than dinosaurs!

Shot through the heart:
an air-rifle pellet pierces
a rose flash-frozen in
liquid nitrogen.

FEB

OF ALL THE MONTHS IN A YEAR, CURSE A FAIR FEBRUARY

RUARY

FEBRUARY 2013

1 FRIDAY

2 SATURDAY

3 SUNDAY

4 MONDAY

5 TUESDAY

6 WEDNESDAY

7 THURSDAY

8 FRIDAY

9 SATURDAY

10 SUNDAY

11 MONDAY

12 TUESDAY

13 WEDNESDAY

14 Valentine's Day
THURSDAY

15 FRIDAY

16 SATURDAY

17 SUNDAY

18 MONDAY

19 TUESDAY

20 WEDNESDAY

21 THURSDAY

22 FRIDAY

23 SATURDAY

24 SUNDAY

25 MONDAY

26 TUESDAY

27 WEDNESDAY

28 THURSDAY

Bird of the Month

Bewick's Swan
(Cygnus columbianus)

LENGTH: 115–140 cm

RANGE: Widespread in the northern hemisphere; known as the Tundra Swan in the U.S.

Thomas Bewick was a wood engraver and naturalist. He wrote The History of British Birds *from 1797 to 1804. The word* swan *is Old English and similar to the Germanic and Scandinavian versions of the word and related to the Latin* sonus *'sound', possibly in reference to the bird's call.*

Sudoku Challenge

7	4			9			2	5
		4		5				
	3		2		8		1	
		1				6		
	6						9	
		5				3		
	8		5		6		3	
			1		7			
6	5			4			8	7

Answers on p. 156

125 YEARS OF NATIONAL GEOGRAPHIC

Krithi Karanth, a conservation biologist based in Bangalore, India, received the 10,000th research grant to be awarded by the National Geographic Society in December 2011.

EXPLORING THE WORLD

In 1890 Israel C. Russell led the Society's first expedition to map Mount St. Elias in Alaska. Since then, the National Geographic Society has funded over 10,000 grants for research and expeditions to almost every corner of the Earth. Formalised as the Committee for Research and Exploration in 1916, the CRE gathers a distinguished board to review applications and grant funds to scientists worldwide. After conducting fieldwork, grantees send reports to Society headquarters. Some of their results may be featured in National Geographic publications, on the website, or on television. Some of the most well-known grant recipients include Jane Goodall, Bob Ballard, Paul Sereno and Mike Fay. Recently the CRE awarded its 10,000th grant in December 2011 to Krithi Karanth, a 32-year-old conservation biologist based in Bangalore, India. ■

The Society's very first grant was given to I. C. Russell in 1890 to explore and map Mount St. Elias in Alaska.

February Constellation

Overhead in the late winter, sky watchers can see a group of stars long identified as twins: the famous brothers Castor and Pollux. The feet of the twins of Gemini are just northeast of Betelgeuse, the bright star at the shoulder of Orion's upraised arm.

GEMINI

MAKEUP: 13 stars
BEST VIEWED: Feb/Mar
LOCATION: Winter, southeast quadrant
SIZE IN THE SKY: ✋
ALPHA STAR: Castor
DEEP SKY OBJECT: NGC 2392, Clownface Nebula

Mythology The alpha and beta stars are named after the twins born of Leda and Zeus. They served as shipmates with Jason on the *Argo*. Castor and Pollux also had a sister named Helen, whose beauty instigated the Trojan War.

About At the heads of the twins, Castor and Pollux are the alpha and beta stars in the constellation. The annual Geminids is one of the more impressive meteor showers. An interesting feature in Gemini is the Clownface Nebula, a disc-shaped blue-green planetary nebula. Photographs through large telescopes reveal the source of the name; a ring of light around a central star alternately seen as the nose of the clown. Messier 35 resides near the three 'foot stars' of Gemini. This open star cluster—best viewed through binoculars or a telescope—consists of hundreds of stars. It is about 20 light-years across and about 2,700 light-years distant. ■

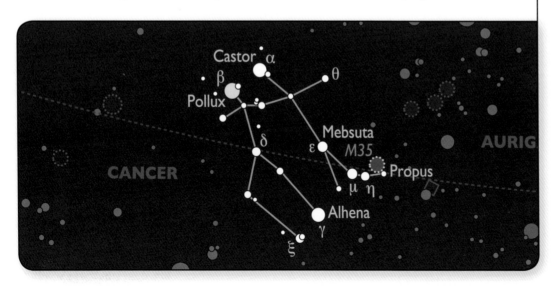

Magnetic Moon

Unlike Earth, the moon has no global magnetic field, but patches of the satellite's surface are magnetic. Why's that? According to new models, these unusually magnetic pockets come from an asteroid that slammed into the moon when it had a magnetic field, billions of years ago.

Zebras' Anti-Bloodsucking Stripes

Conventional wisdom says a zebra's black-and-white stripes camouflage the animal in tall grass—the better to evade the colourblind lion. But a new study says the pattern scrambles the vision of a tinier biter: the bloodsucking horsefly.

BLOODSUCKING HORSEFLY

A zebra can't change its stripes any more than a leopard can change its spots, but according to new research it wouldn't want to—the stripes deter flies.

Horseflies, the females of which feed on blood, are attracted to polarised light—light waves that are oriented in a particular direction and that we experience as glare. This glare most likely lures the insect because it resembles light reflected off water, where they lay their eggs.

On horses, black fur reflects polarised light better than brown or white, as evolutionary ecologist Susanne Åkesson and colleagues found in a previous study.

The researchers therefore assumed that zebra coats, with their mixture of light and dark stripes, would be less attractive to flies than those of black horses but more than those of white horses.

But after experiments in which the team measured the number of horseflies that became trapped on gluey, striped boards or models of horses, the team found that zebra stripes are the best fly repellent—and the narrower the stripes the better. The results may help explain why zebras' skinniest stripes are on their faces and legs. 'That's also the place where you have the thinnest skin,' said Åkesson, of Sweden's Lunds University.

But why is striped skin more effective than white, which has the lowest reflectivity of polarised light? The black-and-white pattern, Åkesson said, turns out to be 'ideal in its function of disrupting this signal of reflected polarised light'.

Because the coat reflects light in alternately polarised and nonpolarised patterns, the zebra 'is more difficult to single out relative to the surroundings'. It is, in effect, camouflaged to flies as well as to big cats. ∎

STRANGE ... BUT TRUE!

Zookeepers are bitten more often by zebras than by tigers.

Geography Q&A

Q **1** What term is used for the often triangular-shaped deposit of sediment sometimes found at the mouth of a river?

Q **2** What is the term for the point on Earth's surface directly above the place where an earthquake originates?

← **Q** **3** A moraine is made up of soil, rocks and other materials that have been deposited by the action of what kind of physical feature?

Answers on p. 154

BIOLOGY

Mix, Match, Morph

It's a dog's world. For reasons both practical and whimsical, man's best friend has been artificially evolved into the most diverse animal on the planet—a staggering achievement, given that most of the 350 to 400 dog breeds in existence have been around for only a couple hundred years. Breeders have fast-forwarded the normal pace of evolution by combining traits from disparate dogs and accentuating them by breeding those offspring that have the largest hints of the desired attributes. Surprisingly, recent canine genomic research has revealed that the vast mosaic of dog shapes, colours and sizes is decided largely by changes in just a few gene regions. The difference between the dachshund's diminutive body, for instance, and a rottweiler's massive one hangs on the sequence of a single gene. The wiener dog's stumpy legs and a greyhound's sleek ones are defined by another lone gene. 'The story that is emerging,' says Robert Wayne, a biologist at UCLA, 'is that the diversity in domestic dogs derives from a small genetic tool kit.' ■

There are more types of dog than of any other kind of animal. Artificial breeding techniques have helped dogs evolve into the planet's most diverse creature.

Glowing Blue Waves Explained

The biological light, or bioluminescence, in the waves is the product of marine microbes called phytoplankton, and now scientists think they know how some of these life-forms create their brilliant blue glow. Various species of phytoplankton are known to bioluminesce, and their lights can be seen in oceans all around the world, said marine biologist and bioluminescence expert Woodland Hastings of Harvard University.

'I've been across the Atlantic and Pacific, and I've never seen a spot that wasn't bioluminescent or a night that [bioluminescence] couldn't be seen,' Hastings said.

The most common type of marine bioluminescence is generated by phytoplankton known as dinoflagellates. A recent study co-authored by Hastings has for the first time identified a special channel in the dinoflagellate cell membrane that responds to electrical signals—offering a potential mechanism for how the algae create their unique illumination. ∎

Phytoplankton create a brilliant blue glow known as bioluminescence, visible here as the tide hits the beach on Vaadhoo Island, Raa Atoll, Maldives.

Grow Your Own Organs

The burgeoning field of regenerative medicine seeks nothing less than to provide patients with replacement body parts. Here, the parts are not steel pins and such. They are the real thing: living cells, tissue and even organs.

Regenerative medicine is still a mostly experimental enterprise, with clinical applications limited to such procedures as growing sheets of skin to graft onto burns and wounds. But the prospects go much further. As long ago as 1999, a research group at North Carolina's Wake Forest Institute for Regenerative Medicine implanted a patient with a laboratory-grown bladder. The team has continued to generate an array of other tissues and organs, from kidneys to salivary glands to ears.

In 2007, a team led by orthopedic surgeon Cato Laurencin, then at the University of Virginia, reported on a tissue-engineered ligament that could allow patients to recover more quickly and fully from one of the most common types of knee injury: the torn anterior cruciate ligament (ACL). Laurencin's ACL was made of braided synthetic microfibres 'seeded' with actual ACL cells. Tested in rabbits, the scaffold, a supporting framework, promoted new blood vessel and collagen growth within 12 weeks.

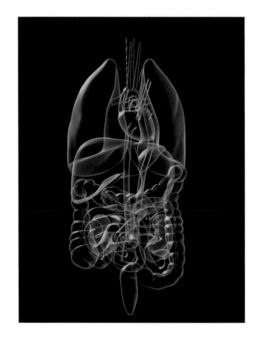

The ability to grow replacement body parts, such as kidneys, is a very important step forward for medical science, as there are never enough donor organs for all those who need them.

Also working in animal models, other researchers have made important strides in testing therapies based on stem cells, which multiply rapidly and can differentiate into a variety of cell types. These repair cells may eventually be deployed to regrow cardiac muscle damaged by heart attack, or to replace nerve cells in victims of spinal-cord injury.

The genesis of this approach goes back to the early 20th century and the first successful transplantations of donated human soft tissue, bone and corneas. As much as transplant medicine has progressed, it suffers from an intractable problem that regenerative medicine might one day sweep aside: there are not enough donor organs for people who need them, so many patients die while waiting for an organ. Another advantage of regenerative medicine is that the body's immune system will not reject tissues grown from a patient's own cells. ∎

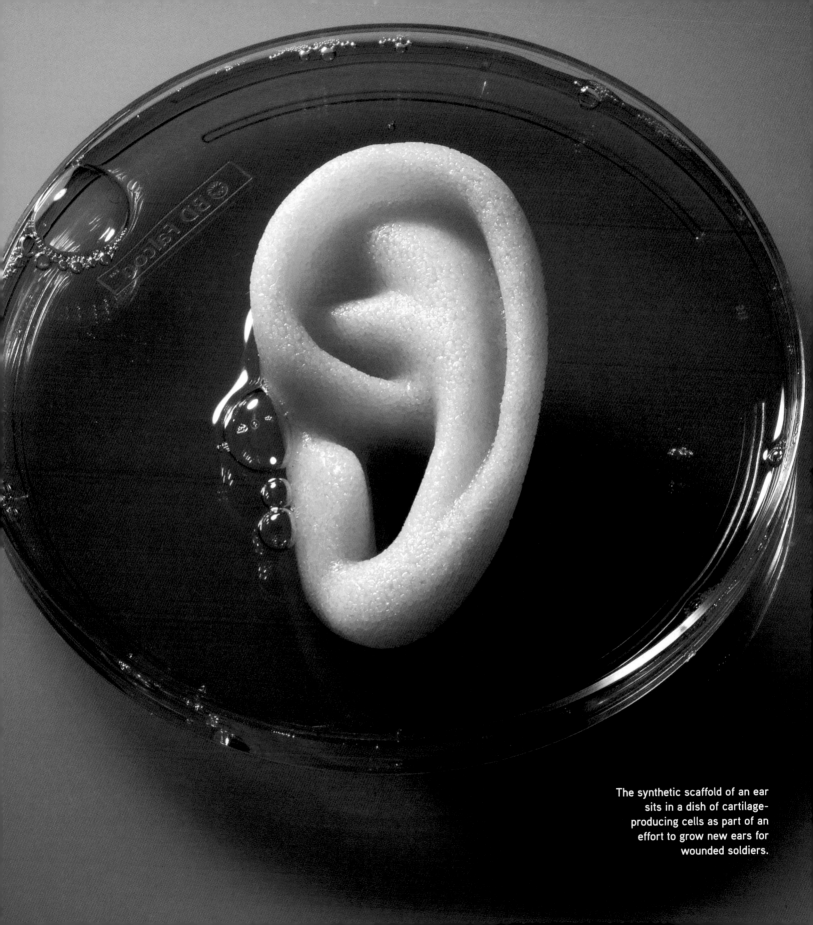

The synthetic scaffold of an ear sits in a dish of cartilage-producing cells as part of an effort to grow new ears for wounded soldiers.

The happy couple: A pair of blue herons prepare their nest for the female to lay between three and six eggs.

St. Valentine's Day

The day we traditionally give flowers and chocolate to our sweethearts has its origins in an ancient Roman festival called Lupercalia. Two youths of noble lineage were anointed with the blood of a sacrificed goat. They proceeded to go romping through the streets of Rome, lashing at young maidens with goatskin thongs known as *februa* (from the Latin for 'to purify' and the root of 'February'). The ritual was meant to protect the animals and crops and to ensure the fertility of both animals and owners. With the spread of Christianity, pagan traditions mingled with Christian, and by the fifth century A.D. the February festival had acquired the name of a saint. ◾

Herb of the Month

Butterbur

TRADITIONAL USES:
Migraine headaches, seasonal allergies

How to Use Butterbur has been used medicinally for at least 2,000 years. The ancient Greeks used it to treat asthma. In medieval Europe, infusions of butterbur roots or leaves were a remedy for treating coughs, hoarseness, bronchial infections and urinary tract complaints and to expel intestinal worms. It was given to lower fever and calm intestinal ailments. In the 1600s, fresh butterbur leaves went into poultices that were applied to swellings, painful joints, cramped muscles, rashes, wounds and other irritations. People even smoked dried butterbur roots or leaves to relieve nagging coughs. The number of ailments for which butterbur is used in modern herbal medicine is considerable. One of its primary therapeutic applications is in treating migraine headaches. ◾

Strange . . . but True: Marine Animals

❶ Octopuses have three hearts.

❷ Certain sharks walk on their fins underwater.

❸ A goldfish will turn grey if kept in the dark for a long time.

❹ A group of jellyfish is called a smack.

❺ Some fish eggs hatch in the dad's mouth.

❻ Some sea stars break off their own arms when frightened.

❼ A shark can live for six weeks without eating.

❽ A baby humpback whale drinks up to 600 litres of milk each day.

❾ A bottlenose dolphin has a brain bigger than a human's.

❿ You can tell the age of some fish by counting the rings on their scales.

A Ferris wheel lights up the night sky at the Kansas State Fair, U.S.A.

COMES IN LIKE A LION, GOES OUT LIKE A LAMB

MARCH

MARCH 2013

1 St David's Day (Wales)
FRIDAY

2 SATURDAY

3 SUNDAY

4 MONDAY

5 TUESDAY

6 WEDNESDAY

7 THURSDAY

8 FRIDAY

9 SATURDAY

10 SUNDAY

11 MONDAY

12 TUESDAY

13 WEDNESDAY

14 THURSDAY

15 The Ides of March
FRIDAY

16 SATURDAY

17 St Patrick's Day
SUNDAY

18 MONDAY

19 TUESDAY

20 First Day of Spring
WEDNESDAY

21 THURSDAY

22 FRIDAY

23 SATURDAY

24 SUNDAY

25 MONDAY

26 TUESDAY

27 WEDNESDAY

28 THURSDAY

29 Good Friday
FRIDAY

30 SATURDAY

31 Easter Sunday
SUNDAY

FOR THE BIRDS
Bird of the Month

European Turtle Dove
(Sterptopelia turtur)

LENGTH: 24–29 cm

RANGE: Breeds in Europe, migrates to Africa

Dove has its origins in the Germanic word dubo *meaning 'dark-coloured bird'. Turtle comes from the Latin word* turtur *and was originally used by Pliny in reference to a dove.*

GEO PUZZLE
Sudoku Challenge

	6		9		8		3	
7				5				8
9		1				5		4
3	1	9				4	7	5
				4				
4	2	8				3	1	6
1		5				8		3
2				3				1
	9		1		5		4	

Answers on p. 156

Divers help to prepare the Deepsea Challenger submarine as it descends on a test dive of 26,000 feet (8,000 metres).

REACHING THE MARIANA TRENCH

Filmmaker and explorer James Cameron emerges from his sub after his record dive.

On 26 March 2012, James Cameron's 'vertical torpedo' submarine broke the surface of the western Pacific about 300 miles (500 kilometres) southwest of Guam, carrying the National Geographic explorer and filmmaker back from the Mariana Trench's Challenger Deep—Earth's deepest, and perhaps most alien, realm. The first human to reach the 6.8-mile-deep (11-kilometre-deep) undersea valley solo, Cameron arrived at the bottom with the technology to collect scientific data, specimens and images unthinkable in 1960, when the only other manned Challenger Deep dive took place. Among the 2.5-storey-tall sub's tools are a sediment sampler, a robotic claw, a 'slurp gun' for sucking up small sea creatures for study at the surface and temperature, salinity and pressure gauges. ∎

March Constellation

Spring is galaxy-hunting season. Earth's position relative to the Milky Way has shifted so that the core of the galaxy lies near the horizon in the east. We look out into deep space with a better view of elusive night sky objects. Ursa Major swings highest above Polaris in spring.

HYDRA

MAKEUP: 17 stars
BEST VIEWED: Mar/Apr
LOCATION: Spring, southwest quadrant
SIZE IN THE SKY: 🖐🖐🖐🖐🖐
ALPHA STAR: Alphard
DEEP SKY OBJECT: M83, spiral galaxy

Mythology When Hydra battled with Hercules, the multi-headed serpent appeared invincible when, as Hercules chopped off each head, more grew in its place. Finally, Hydra was defeated when each stump was burned to prevent the growth of new heads.

About This monster occupies a larger strip of sky than any other constellation as it winds its way from Libra to Cancer. Its line of stars is led by a kite-shaped cluster, representing the serpent's head. Spring provides the clearest view.

Alphard, the 'heart of the serpent', is Hydra's brightest star and can be located by looking just east of a line traced from Regulus in Leo to Sirius in Canis Major. With a tail that drops close to the southern horizon from mid-northern latitudes, Hydra does not match its size with luminosity: All its dispersed members are magnitude 3 or dimmer, with the exception of two. ■

Beware the Ides

Thanks to Shakespeare, 15 March, the Ides of March, is forever linked with the 44 B.C. assassination of Julius Caesar. Originally it signalled a date to settle debts. The word's Latin roots mean 'divide', and the date sought to split the month at the rise of the full moon.

World's Smallest Chameleon

Match-tip tiny, *Brookesia micra* is the smallest of four new chameleon species found on the African island country of Madagascar. With an average adult length of just 2.9 centimetres from snout to tail, *B. micra* is among the tiniest reptiles in the world.

ACTUAL SIZE 2.9 CM

Shown here perched on a match tip, the *Brookesia micra* is the smallest of four new species of chameleon found on the island of Madagascar.

Scientists think the diminutive new chameleon species might represent extreme cases of island dwarfism, whereby organisms shrink in size due to limited resources on islands. 'The extreme miniaturisation of these dwarf reptiles might be accompanied by numerous specialisations of the body plan, and this constitutes a promising field for future research,' study leader Frank Glaw of Germany's Zoological State Collection said in a statement.

The small sizes of the four new chameleon species make them especially vulnerable to habitat destruction, and some of their names were chosen to reflect this. The latter part of *B. desperata*'s name, for example, means 'desperate' in Latin.

'Its habitat is in truth barely protected and subject to numerous human-induced environmental problems resulting in severe habitat destruction, thus threatening the survival of the species,' the scientists write. Another species was named *B. tristis,* or 'sorrowful'—a reference to 'the fact that the entire known range of this species suffers from severe deforestation and habitat destruction'.

Although the four new chameleon species look very similar, genetic analyses suggest the reptiles are in fact different species, according to the study. Scientists from Germany and the United States published their findings in the journal *PLoS One* in February 2012. ∎

STRANGE . . . BUT TRUE!

The world's lightest mammal, the bumblebee bat, weighs about as much as two M&M's.

Geography Q & A

Q ❶ The Vistula River and Bialowieza National Park—northern Europe's largest virgin forest and home to the European bison—are in which country?

Q ❷ What city is home to the building pictured on the left, designed by famed architect Antoni Gaudí?

Q ❸ To visit the ruins of Persepolis, an ancient ceremonial capital of Persia, you would have to travel to what present-day country?

Answers on p. 154

Great Tree Survey

The news from the planet's forests has been surprisingly good lately, at least compared with the news of a decade or two ago. Globally, according to a United Nations report that came out in 2010, the rate at which forests are destroyed—logged or cleared to make way for farms or mines—was nearly 20 per cent lower from 2000 to 2010 than it had been in the previous decade. Huge tree-planting programs reduced the net loss of forest even further. But vast areas are still being slashed, including each year a Switzerland-sized area of previously undisturbed, ecologically precious 'primary' forest. Rough estimates indicate deforestation still contributes around four billion tons of planet-warming CO_2 to the atmosphere each year, an eighth of the human total. ■

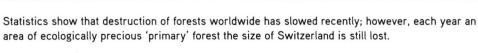

Statistics show that destruction of forests worldwide has slowed recently; however, each year an area of ecologically precious 'primary' forest the size of Switzerland is still lost.

The Moon's Molten Core

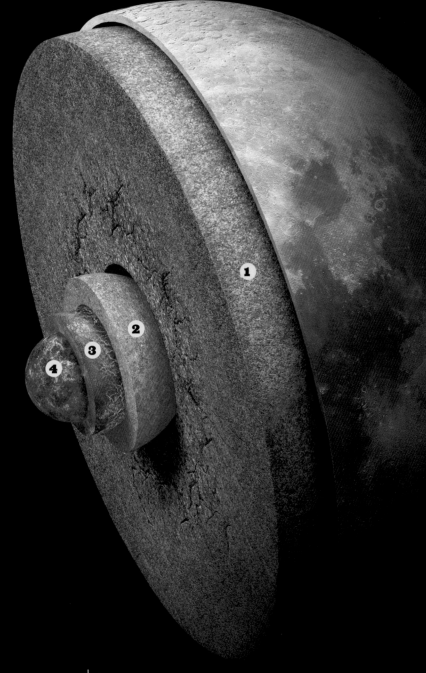

When Apollo astronauts visited the moon, they drilled no deeper than three metres. Yet the instruments they left behind are helping us learn even today about the inner life of our celestial neighbour. The latest look at seismic data from four decades ago confirms that deep inside this cold, dry satellite is a hot, liquid core.

'The molten core tells us a lot about the evolution of the moon,' says NASA's Renee Weber, who studied readings dating from 1969 to 1977, only a quarter of which had been analysed since the Apollo missions. The power of modern computers enabled Weber and her colleagues to examine the remainder, with a focus on deep moonquakes. Like the Earth, the moon has a centre consisting of liquid and solid layers, the innermost being the hottest yet solid due to intense pressure. But whereas the Earth's core is convecting—that is, dynamic, giving rise to plate tectonics, volcanic activity and a magnetic field—the moon is thought to be stagnant.

The liquid present in the outer core suggests the moon may have been entirely molten when it formed 4.5 billion years ago, says Weber. 'Even though the Earth and moon formed at similar times, the moon is smaller, so it has lost heat and energy faster.' At some point the lunar core may have convected as well. How do we know? Magnetic traces on surface samples brought back by the astronauts. ■

THE INTERIOR	①	②	③	④
NAME	Mantle	Partial melt zone	Outer core (liquid)	Inner core (solid)
DEPTH FROM SURFACE	25 miles	780 miles	875 miles	930 miles
CONTENTS	Includes olivine, peridotite and garnet	Peridotite, titanium-rich silicate melt	Liquid iron alloy	Solid iron alloy
TEMPERATURE	1,600 kelvins (1,327 °C)	1,650 kelvins (1,377 °C)	1,700 kelvins (1,427 °C)	1,710 kelvins (1, 437 °C)

Area 51's Secret Plane Crash

After a rash of declassifications, details of Cold War workings at the Area 51 Nevada base, which to this day does not officially exist, are coming to light— including never-before-released images of an A-12 crash and its cover-up.

Area 51 was created so that U.S. Cold Warriors with the highest security clearances could pursue cutting-edge aeronautical projects away from prying eyes. During the 1950s and '60s Area 51's top-secret OXCART programme developed the A-12 as the successor to the U-2 spy plane. Nearly undetectable to radar, the A-12 could fly at 2,200 miles an hour (3,540 kilometres an hour)—fast enough to cross the continental U.S. in 70 minutes. From 27,400 metres, the plane's cameras could capture 30-centimetre-long objects on the ground below.

But pushing the limits came with risks, and a catastrophic 1963 crash of an A-12 based out of Area 51. A rapid government cover-up removed nearly all public traces of the wrecked A-12. Things went horribly wrong for test pilot Ken Collins (flying under his Area 51 code name Ken Colmar) when testing the plane's subsonic engines at low altitude.

There is such a shroud of secrecy surrounding the Area 51 testing site that the U.S. government doesn't even formally acknowledge its existence.

At 7,620 metres, 'the aeroplane pitched up and went up and got inverted and went into a flat incipient spin,' Collins says in the National Geographic Channel documentary *Area 51 Declassified*. From such a position, 'you just can't recover. So I thought I'd better eject, so

I ejected down, because I was upside down.' U.S. officials later asked Collins to undergo hypnosis and treatments of sodium pentothal (a 'truth drug') to confirm he had relayed every detail of the incident truthfully and correctly.

After pilot Ken Collins had parachuted to the ground, he was stunned to be greeted by three civilians in a pickup, who offered to take him to the wreckage of his plane. Instead, Collins got them to drive him in the opposite direction, by telling them the plane had a nuclear weapon on board—a prearranged cover story to keep the Area 51 craft a secret.

Soon a team of government agents appeared to direct a complete cleanup— and cover-up—operation. By the next morning, recovery crews had begun loading the wreckage onto trucks for the return trip to Area 51 in Nevada. No one else approached the wreck site or even learned of the crash during the next half century. ■

DECLASSIFIED!

1 A crane hoists A-12 debris onto a flatbed truck at the site of the 1963 A-12 crash in Utah, U.S.A.

2 A government 'sanitation' team uses heavy equipment, including bulldozers and cranes, to remove all traces of the A-12 spy plane from the 1963 crash site in the Utah desert.

3 Suspended upside down, a titanium A-12 spy-plane prototype is prepped for radar testing at Area 51 in the late 1950s.

Desert winds have helped sand dunes reclaim this abandoned house in Kolmanskop, Namibia, once a thriving settlement for diamond miners.

The Four-Leaf Clover

According to Irish legends and Julius Caesar, the Druids of the British Isles and Gaul were the first to believe in the luck of the four-leaf clover. The Druids were an ancient Celtic priesthood who held religious rites in sacred oak groves. The Druids' oak grove rituals involved collecting four-leaf clovers and mistletoe. It is unclear how the plants were used, but their rarity likely gave them elevated status. Druids may have believed that having a four-leaf clover gave them the ability to see witches and devils, and thus the power to avoid them. Also, the four-leaf clover is cross-shaped, which was a magic symbol, representing, among other things, the cardinal directions. ■

Herb of the Month

Liquorice

TRADITIONAL USES:
Sore throat, cough, heartburn, gastritis

History No one knows who first discovered that the tangled, fleshy roots of liquorice possess an intense sweetness. But evidence of liquorice's use is widespread in ancient cultures. Archaeologists found bundles of licorice root sealed inside the 3,000-year-old tomb of Tutankhamen, presumably so the Egyptian king could brew *mai sus* in the afterlife, a sweet drink still enjoyed in Egypt today. The species known to both the ancient Egyptians and ancient Greeks was *Glycyrrhiza glabra,* commonly called European liquorice. But there was more to liquorice's appeal than its sweetness. Liquorice root was also prized medicinally, primarily as a remedy for digestive and respiratory ailments. ■

Strange . . . but True: Earth

❶ The Earth spins so fast that someone standing at the Equator is travelling at about 1,000 miles an hour.

❷ More than a thousand Earths could fit inside Jupiter.

❸ If you travelled as fast as a car on the motorway, it would take nearly three days and nights to reach the Earth's core.

❹ Earth's temperature rises slightly during a full moon.

❺ All of the people on Earth could crowd into half of Belgium.

❻ If you are 12 years old on Earth, you'd be about 6 on Mars.

❼ It takes 8 minutes and 19 seconds for light to travel from the sun to Earth.

❽ There are more species of beetle on Earth than any other type of creature.

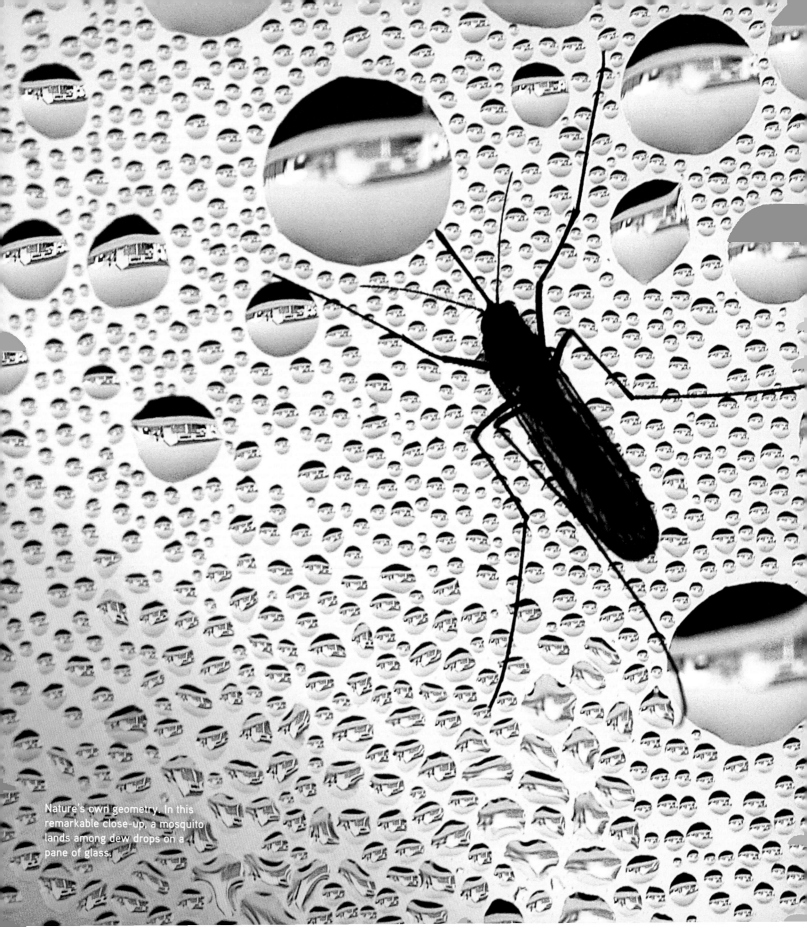

Nature's own geometry. In this remarkable close-up, a mosquito lands among dew drops on a pane of glass.

SWEET APRIL SHOWERS, DO SPRING MAY FLOWERS

APRIL

1 MONDAY — April Fools Day/Easter Monday

2 TUESDAY ◑

3 WEDNESDAY

4 THURSDAY

5 FRIDAY

6 SATURDAY

7 SUNDAY

8 MONDAY

9 TUESDAY

10 WEDNESDAY ●

11 THURSDAY

12 FRIDAY

13 SATURDAY

14 SUNDAY

15 MONDAY

16 TUESDAY

17 WEDNESDAY

18 THURSDAY ◐

19 FRIDAY

20 SATURDAY

21 SUNDAY

22 MONDAY

23 TUESDAY — St George's Day (England)

24 WEDNESDAY

25 THURSDAY ○

26 FRIDAY

27 SATURDAY

28 SUNDAY

29 MONDAY

30 TUESDAY

Bird of the Month

Corncrake *(Crex crex)*

LENGTH: 27 cm

RANGE: Europe; accidental in eastern North America

'Corn' is in reference to the bird's keenness for grain fields (wheat was once called corn in England). Crex is a Latin and Greek word for a long-legged bird, but was given to this rail in imitation of its call.

Sudoku Challenge

	9						7	
	4		8		7		2	
		2				1		
8		6	2		9	7		1
			7		8			
7		9	6		1	2		4
		5				9		
	6		4		2		3	
	2						4	

Answers on p. 156

The wonder of the frozen planet. A giant iceberg floats on the waters of east Greenland.

REACHING THE NORTH POLE

In 1907 the Society awarded a grant to Commander Robert E. Peary in support of his attempt to reach the North Pole. Peary had already made several treks north, and for these pioneering explorations the Society presented him with the first Hubbard Medal, its highest honour. Standing on feet crippled by frostbite, the determined Peary accepted the medal from President Theodore Roosevelt and vowed to reach his goal.

Robert E. Peary is recognised as having been the first person to reach the North Pole, despite claims by Frederick A. Cook.

Peary and his crew reached the top of the world on 6 April 1909. A dispute quickly erupted. Frederick A. Cook claimed to have reached the Pole four days earlier, but he presented little evidence. After a Society committee examined Peary's records and concluded that he, at least, had reached the spot, nearly every geographical body in the world agreed. But the dispute still lingers. ■

April Constellation

Ursa Major, or the Great Bear, is one of the dominant shapes in the northern sky, including the seven-star asterism known as the Plough (also called the Big Dipper in the U.S.). It is one of the most ancient constellations, associated with stories that have cut across many cultures.

URSA MAJOR

MAKEUP: 20 stars
BEST VIEWED: Mar/Apr
LOCATION: Spring, centre of chart
SIZE IN THE SKY: ✋✋
ALPHA STAR: Dubhe
DEEP SKY OBJECT: Mizar & Alcor

Mythology In Greek mythology the Great Bear represents the nymph Callisto who was transformed into a bear by Hera, enraged after discovering that Hera's husband Zeus had impregnated her. Callisto's son, Arcas, mistakenly tried to kill her while hunting. Zeus intervened and placed them in the sky.

About From the north, over the course of the year, the Great Bear appears to run in a circle with its back to Polaris, the North Star. March and April mark the season when the Bear is highest in the sky. The Bear hosts a pair of galaxies—M81 and M82—best seen with binoculars. The easily identified Plough represents the rear torso and tail of the Bear, with the other stars mapping out its long nose and legs. It's among the few constellations with a close-to-literal overall shape. ■

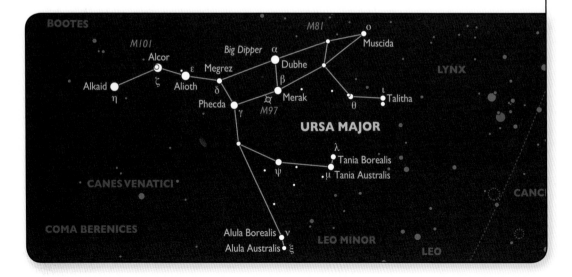

BOOTES
M101
Alcor
Alkaid
η
ζ
ε Megrez
Alioth
δ
Phecda
γ
M97
Big Dipper α
Dubhe
β
Merak
ι Talitha
θ
M81
ο
Muscida
LYNX
URSA MAJOR
λ
Tania Borealis
ψ
μ Tania Australis
CANES VENATICI
CANC
COMA BERENICES
Alula Borealis ν
Alula Australis ξ
LEO MINOR
LEO

Mother of Invention

In 1953, Japanese researchers observed Imo, an alpha-female Japanese macaque, dip a sweet potato into water to clean sand from its skin before eating it. Soon, other members of her troupe caught on. Imo's generation passed the skill to their offspring, and monkeys in this area of Japan still use it today.

Bacteria Lend a Helping Hand

The surface of human skin is crowded with bacteria that would, if your immune system allowed it, cause serious infection. But researchers at the University of California, San Diego, have discovered that one bacterium in that mix, *Staphylococcus epidermidis*, may actually help fine-tune the immune system.

To do its good work, *Staphylococcus epidermidis* (a close cousin of methicillin-resistant *Staphylococcus aureus,* or MRSA) deploys a molecule that blocks aggressive inflammatory agents. If unchecked, those agents would ignite a rashy reaction around even a minor scrape. 'Good' staph stays good only if locked outside by the skin's multiple defences, though. If that germ finds a way into a weakened body—on a surgical implant, for example—it can ignite a potentially fatal infection.

Staphylococcus epidermidis is not the only helpful bacteria. In fact, your skin has loads of bacteria working in its favour. On the microbial level, for example, a person's underarms are akin to lush rain forests brimming with diversity—

and that's a good thing! A 2009 study revealed a 'topographic map' of human skin. Most of our skin is like an arid desert, said study co-author Julia Segre, of the National Human Genome Research Institute in Bethesda, Maryland, U.S.A. 'But as you walk through this desert you encounter an oasis, which is the inside of your nose,' she said. 'You encounter a stream, which is a moist crease. [These] areas are like habitats rich in diversity.' And like the 'friendly' bugs in the human digestive system, these native bacteria of the epidermis promote skin health and could even help scientists find new ways to treat skin diseases.

Germophobes needn't freak out. Segre stresses that many of the microbes are 'healthy bacteria' that keep our largest organ in good condition. For example, germs that live in naturally oily regions, such as the outside of the nose, feed

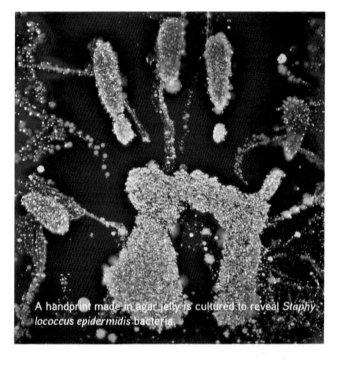

A handprint made in agar jelly is cultured to reveal *Staphylococcus epidermidis* bacteria.

on the skin's lipids and produce natural moisturisers to prevent skin from becoming chapped. 'People are eating probiotic yoghurts to promote [beneficial] bacteria growth in the gut, but we want to sterilise the skin,' Serge noted. 'We should think about proper sanitation with the skin, but not sterilisation. There are good bacteria that really promote healthy skin.' ■

STRANGE ... BUT TRUE!

Your tongue print is as unique as your fingerprints.

Geography Q&A

Q 1 The samba, which was originally brought from Africa, is a dance that was adapted and is highly popular on which other continent?

Q 2 In ancient times the papyrus plant, used for making paper, grew along the Nile River Delta in which country?

Q 3 Afrikaners are the descendants of European settlers who mostly live in which present-day African country?

Answers on p. 154

Twenty-nine Names, Same Plant

In 1753 Swedish naturalist Carl Linnaeus published *Species Plantarum*, a book describing some 6,000 plant species that became the foundation of modern plant nomenclature. The list of names has since grown to 1.05 million, but of those, only around 300,000 are now confirmed to be unique species. Nearly half a million others, it turns out, are redundant.

The scientific moniker for English oak has 314 synonyms, the common daisy (left) 29 and the giant sequoia 18. Those are just a few identified so far in the Plant List, a working database created in 2010 by the Missouri Botanical Garden and London's Kew Gardens after years of vetting. 'It's like people. We have different eye colours, shapes and sizes, but we're all people,' says botanist Bob Magill. 'There's huge variation within a species.'

An illustration shows all 29 scientific names for the common daisy. The English oak has 314 different names.

Whales Hunt Using Sonar 'Beam'

Toothed whales target moving prey with a constantly shifting, tightly focused sonar beam, a new study says. All toothed whales and dolphins echolocate, clicking loudly via special nasal structures and listening for echoes bouncing off objects. This skill is crucial in the dark ocean, where the mammals' vision is of little use. New experiments show that whales can focus their clicks into a specific type of sonar beam to efficiently track fast-moving prey.

'The bottom line is echolocation is how these animals make their living,' said study leader Laura Kloepper, a zoologist at the University of Hawaii in Honolulu. 'Not only do they have to locate fish, they have to discriminate fish and figure out what kind of fish it is.'

As recently as 2008, 'not much attention was paid to the incredible flexibility' of echolocating whales, noted Dorian Houser, director of Biology and Bioacoustic Research at the National Marine Mammal Foundation. The new study contributes 'to our growing knowledge about the ability of [the whale] to control its echolocation beam by changing its width and frequency content,' Houser said. Plenty of echolocation mysteries remain, however—for example, how whales can hear properly even while clicking incredibly loudly (the focus of the study team's next project).

'The more information we obtain on their ability to manipulate the beam,' Houser said, 'the more complicated the story becomes.'

Bizarre 'King of Wasps'

A new species of giant, venomous wasp has been found on the Indonesian island of Sulawesi, scientists say. The five-centimetre-long black insects are shrouded in mystery—all of the wasp specimens caught so far have been dead.

I'm not certain any researcher has ever seen one alive, but they are very bizarre-looking,' said study co-author Lynn Kimsey, an entomologist at the University of California, Davis, who co-discovered the insect. 'It's the extreme version of the [larrine wasp] subfamily they belong to.'

Larrine wasps typically dig nests for their eggs and larvae in open, sandy areas. The adults grow no longer than 2.5 centimetres—making the newly discovered *Megalara garuda* the 'king of wasps', according to the study authors. Female *M. garuda* wasps look like most other wasp species, but the males grow long, sickle-shaped jaws.

The males' flattened faces and large, spiked jaws may be clever adaptations to protect a nest that contains vulnerable larvae, she suggested. 'Other wasps of the same species often rob burrows for food, and parasites try to get in there, too,' she said. 'There's a serious

ACTUAL SIZE 5.1 CM

Newly discovered mega-wasp *Megalara garuda* can grow to be five centimetres long.

advantage to having the nest guarded. This may be how the male helps guarantee his paternity.' In general, 'we don't know what this wasp does,' Kimsey said. 'But it probably feeds its larvae grasshoppers or katydids, like other wasps in its subfamily.'

Kimsey and co-author Michael Ohl, of Berlin's Humboldt University, caught their first glimpse of the new wasp in Indonesia's Museum Zoologicum Bogoriense, where the insects had been kept in storage since 1930. Ohl also found unidentified specimens at the Humboldt Museum in Berlin. On a 2009 expedition, the team found more wasps at a cacao plantation in the southeastern mountains of Sulawesi. In naming *M. garuda*, the team looked to the national symbol of Indonesia: a mythical half-human, half-bird creature in the Hindu religion called Garuda.

Although as many as a hundred thousand species of insect may live on Sulawesi, Kimsey suspects 'only half have names'. But the fates of these species—including the newfound wasp—are in jeopardy. Since the 1960s forests in the region have been increasingly levelled to plant several types of crops. ■

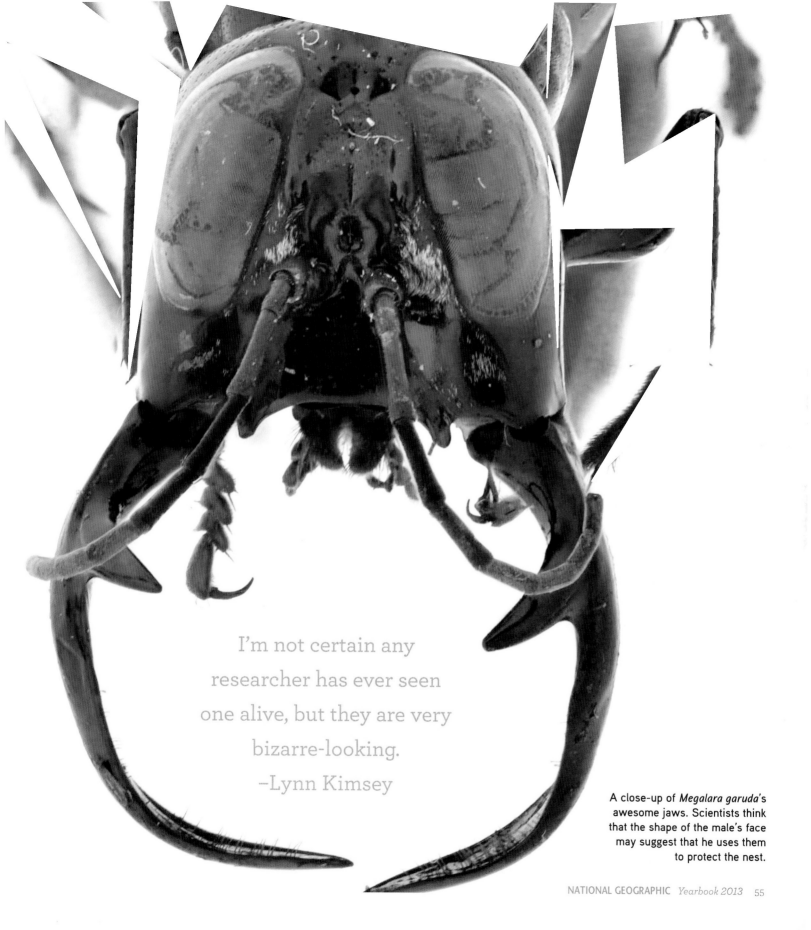

I'm not certain any
researcher has ever seen
one alive, but they are very
bizarre-looking.
–Lynn Kimsey

A close-up of *Megalara garuda*'s
awesome jaws. Scientists think
that the shape of the male's face
may suggest that he uses them
to protect the nest.

The monsoon wind steals
the umbrella of boys playing
in the rain.

April Fools' Day

Theories on the origin of April Fools' Day abound, but the most likely takes it back to 16th-century France. The French accepted the reformed Gregorian calendar in the late 1500s, setting their New Year's Day back from 25 March to 1 January. The old anniversary continued to be celebrated with a week of festivities, topped off by a final day of merriment on 1 April. Pranks were played on those who forgot that the date for New Year's had shifted. The gullible were sent on fool's errands, invited to nonexistent parties and given ridiculous presents. Such people were called *poissons d'Avril* (April fish), because like the newly hatched fish, they were easily caught. The custom did not jump the English Channel until the 18th century; it was known in England as All Fools' Day. ■

Herb of the Month

Echinacea

TRADITIONAL USES: Colds and flu, wounds

History Echinacea's flowers consist of prickly, domed centres encircled by a single layer of lavender-hued petals, the source of the herb's most common name, purple coneflower. The 'cone' is the characteristic perfectly captured by the genus name, as *Echinacea* comes from the Greek *echinos*, meaning 'hedgehog'. Centuries before European settlers arrived in North America, native tribes were using at least three species of echinacea medicinally. The herb was something of a universal remedy to Indians of the Great Plains and neighbouring regions. It was used for more therapeutic purposes than almost any other herb. ■

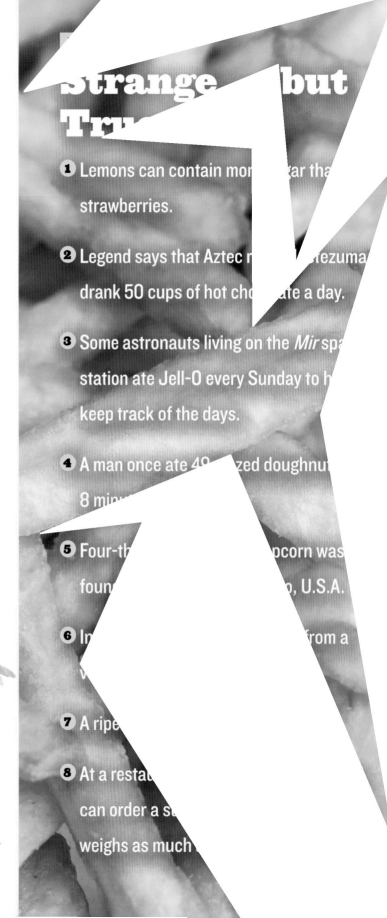

Strange but True

1. Lemons can contain mor[e] [su]gar tha[n] strawberries.

2. Legend says that Aztec [ruler Mo]ntezuma drank 50 cups of hot cho[col]ate a day.

3. Some astronauts living on the *Mir* spa[ce] station ate Jell-O every Sunday to h[elp] keep track of the days.

4. A man once ate 4[9 si]zed doughnut[s in] 8 min[utes].

5. Four-th[ousand-year-old p]opcorn was foun[d in] [New Mexic]o, U.S.A.

6. I[n] [...] from a [...]

7. A ripe [...]

8. At a resta[urant] [...] can order a s[...] weighs as much [...]

A man rides a horse through a bonfire as part of a traditional ceremony held in San Bartolome, Spain, to honour St. Anton, the patron saint of animals.

NE'ER CAST A CLOUT TILL MAY BE OUT

MAY

MAY 2013

1 WEDNESDAY

2 THURSDAY ◑

3 FRIDAY

4 SATURDAY

5 SUNDAY

6 Early May Bank Holiday
MONDAY

7 TUESDAY

8 WEDNESDAY

9 THURSDAY

10 FRIDAY ●

11 SATURDAY

12 SUNDAY

13 MONDAY

14 TUESDAY

15 WEDNESDAY

16 THURSDAY

17 FRIDAY

18 SATURDAY ◑

19 SUNDAY

20 MONDAY

21 TUESDAY

22 WEDNESDAY

23 THURSDAY

24 FRIDAY

25 SATURDAY ○

26 SUNDAY

27 Spring Bank Holiday
MONDAY

28 TUESDAY

29 WEDNESDAY

30 THURSDAY

31 FRIDAY

FOR THE BIRDS
Bird of the Month

Curlew Sandpiper
(Calidris ferruginea)

LENGTH: 19–21 cm
RANGE: Breeds in the Siberian Arctic and winters in Africa and Australasia

Curlew is related to the Old French cour-lierus and Middle English curleu and is in reference to the bird's curved bill. Ferruginea, meaning 'rusty red', comes from the Latin fer-rugo for rust and ferrum for iron and refers to the bird's plumage in mating season.

GEO PUZZLE
Sudoku Challenge

3			4		2			1
	6		3		1		7	
		1	7		9	3		
1				3				7
	3		9		4		2	
8				2				4
	2	5		8	7			
	5		1		3		6	
9			2		6			5

Answers on p. 156

YEARS OF NATIONAL GEOGRAPHIC

An expedition member pushes on towards the south summit of Mount Everest.

AT THE TOP OF THE WORLD

In 1963 the National Geographic Society reached the top of the world. On 22 May Barry Bishop of the magazine staff planted the Society's flag on the summit of Mount Everest. Bishop was a member of the first American team— and one of the first groups—to summit the world's tallest mountain. His feat crowned the Society's 75th anniversary. Science and exploration were expanding at a rapid pace and the National Geographic Society looked for new ways to bring the world to its readers. On 10 September 1965, the Society aired its first television special. *Americans on Everest* made an astonishing impact, receiving the highest ratings of any documentary broadcast up to that time. ■

Boots belonging to British mountaineer George Mallory, who died trying to climb Everest in 1924

May Constellation

Summer puts the Summer Triangle asterism overhead, providing an easy way to mark three of the season's constellations: Lyra, Cygnus and Aquila. Lyra's main star, Vega, will be almost directly overhead, unmistakably bright at magnitude 0.

VIRGO

MAKEUP: 13 stars
BEST VIEWED: May/Jun
LOCATION: Spring, southeast quadrant
SIZE IN THE SKY: ✋
ALPHA STAR: Spica
DEEP SKY OBJECT: M104, Sombrero galaxy

Objects to Look For In 1781, Chares Messier added the Sombrero Galaxy (M104) to his catalogue. The bright and spectacular galaxy is one of the largest in Virgo. The large bulge in the centre looks like a sombrero floating in space. Spanning an area in the sky about ten times that of the full moon, is the Virgo Cluster of galaxies. The gravitational force of this cluster is so strong that it is slowly pulling our galaxy towards it.

About Virgo is the only zodiacal constellation to represent a woman. Spica, located in the ear of wheat she holds in her left hand, is the brightest star in the constellation. This is by far the brightest one in that part of the sky. It is a key star when star hopping. From the end of the handle of the Plough move south in the 'arc to Arcturus', in the constellation Boötes, then 'speed on to Spica' directly beneath it. ■

Cliff Cave Secrets

Archaeologist Mark Aldenderfer set out to find human remains near an ancient settlement in the Himalayas. He discovered a pile of human bones, dating back 2,500 years. Scholars think this find will shed new light on Bon, the indigenous religion that predated Buddhism in ancient Tibet.

Million Years Growth Spurt

Some mammals need roughly 24 million generations to go from mouse-size to elephant-size, a new study says. Using both fossil and living specimens, scientists calculated growth rates for 28 different mammalian groups during the past 65 million years and found that, for mammals, getting bigger takes longer than shrinking.

Scientists discovered that it takes a minimum of 1.6 million generations for mammals to achieve a hundred-fold increase in body size, about 5 million generations for a thousandfold increase, and about 10 million generations for a 5,000-fold increase. For land mammals, odd-toed ungulates—such as horses and rhinos—displayed the fastest maximum rates. Curiously, primates showed the slowest rates among the mammals examined.

'It's a bit of a mystery,' said study leader Alistair Evans, an evolutionary biologist at Australia's Monash University. 'It's a lot

A zebra follows a bull elephant. For a zebra to reach the size of this elephant it would take many more generations than it would for the elephant to shrink to the size of his friend.

harder to make a big primate than it is to make a big rhino or elephant ... There could be many reasons for this, but staying a primate and getting big seems to be very difficult.'

Among all mammals, cetaceans—the group that includes whales and dolphins—experienced the highest rate of body inflation, requiring only about three million generations for a thou-

sandfold size increase. Evans and his team speculate that difference is likely because their body weight is supported by water, which makes growing larger less challenging than on land. For instance, without the buoyancy of water, a whale's internal organs would be crushed by its own weight. The study also found that mammals shrink up to 30 times faster than they increase. ■

STRANGE **. . . BUT TRUE!**

African elephants have ears shaped like Africa.

Geography Q & A

Q **1** People in the most populous Scandinavian country celebrate a festival of lights called St. Lucia Day to mark the start of the Christmas season. Name this country.

Q **2** Sanskrit, preserved in Hindu sacred writings, is an ancient language in which country?

← **Q** **3** The Gold Museum, which contains a large collection of pre-Columbian gold objects, is in the capital city east of the Magdalena River. Name this city.

Answers on p. 154

BOTANY

New 'PortaLoo Flower' Discovered

Discovered on an island off the coast of Madagascar, the newfound plant—*Amorphophallus perrieri*—grows up to 1.5 metres high and blooms once a year with a 'really foul' stench, according to discoverer Greg Wahlert, a postdoctoral researcher in botany at the University of Utah. Lynn Bohs, a biology professor in the same lab as Wahlert, described the smell as a combination of 'rotting roadkill' and a 'Porta Potty'.

The flower adds to the roughly 170 species in the *Amorphophallus* genus, which means 'misshapen penis' in Greek after the phallic shape of the plants' flowers. *A. perrieri* is dormant for much of the year, so Wahlert's discovery is a case of good timing. ■

Not one for the windowsill—the newly discovered *Amorphophallus perrieri* grows to 4.9 feet (1.5 metres) and smells like rotting meat and faeces.

Famous Pharaoh's Twisted Family Tree

King Tutankhamen may be seen as the golden boy of ancient Egypt today, but during his reign he wasn't exactly a strapping sun god. Instead, a new DNA study says, the king was a frail pharaoh, beset by malaria and a bone disorder, his health possibly compromised by his newly discovered incestuous origins. The report is the first DNA study ever conducted with ancient Egyptian royal mummies. It apparently solves several mysteries surrounding Tutankhamen.

'He was not a very strong pharaoh. He was not riding the chariots,' said study team member Carsten Pusch, a geneticist at Germany's University of Tübingen. 'Picture instead a frail, weak boy who had a bit of a club foot and who needed a cane to walk.'

Regarding the revelation that Tut's mother and father were siblings, Pusch said, 'Inbreeding is not an advantage for biological or genetic fitness. Normally the health and immune system are reduced and malformations increase,' he said.

Using DNA samples taken from the mummies' bones, the scientists were able to create a five-generation family tree for the boy pharaoh, including his father, grandfather, mother (although her identity remains a mystery), grandmother and sister. The team's examination of Tutankhamen's body also revealed previously unknown deformations in the king's left foot, caused by the necrosis, or death, of bone tissue. ■

A forensic reconstruction of King Tutankhamen based on facial scans allows us to see how the famous Egyptian king may have looked.

A Bittersweet Poison Dart Frog

It's a discovery perhaps only a frog-licking scientist could make: some toxic frogs secrete sugars and bile acids in addition to their poisons, a new study says.

Now, alongside her father, electrical engineer William Clark, herpetologist Valerie Clark—an unabashed frog lover and occasional frog licker—has co-created and used an electro-stimulation device to help extract chemicals from skin glands without killing the frogs. 'Skinning [was] a standard practice, but in the last couple of decades, improvements in technology have skyrocketed,' said Clark, a former grantee of the National Geographic Society's Committee for Research and Exploration.

For frogs of the *Mantella* genus of Madagascar, the device helped isolate bile acids and sugars never before seen on frog skins. The chemicals had been 'lost in the mush' of ground-up skins in other expeditions, said Clark. The chemical analyses suggest bile acids and sugars exist in roughly the same

The Madagascan painted frog of the *Mantella* genus has the ability to make itself taste unappealing to predators.

amounts but outnumber the mass of poison alkaloids by roughly ten to one on the frogs.

It's still a mystery why the skins should secrete sugars and bile. Clark suspects the sugars—obtained via the ants the frogs eat—may have a protective function in the amphibians' damp, mouldy environments. As for the bile acids, she imagines they may help explain the frogs' immunity to the ant-borne poisons, as well as how the poisons get from ingested ants to the frogs' skins without harming the amphibians. Physiologist Alan Hofmann thinks the discovery of bile acids on poison-frog skin is a first. 'Ordinarily they're kept in the digestive tract,' said Hofmann, of the University of California, San Diego, who wasn't part of the new study.

The only other animals known to excrete bile acids are lampreys, and those fish seem to use the acids as pheromones, a form of chemical communication. In poison frogs, the bile may be just one more weapon in an already toxic arsenal, Hofmann said. Bile acids are 'terribly bitter', so they may help make the frog unappetising to predators. ■

Scientists are investigating how frogs like the Golden Mantella, pictured here, are able to secrete bile from their skin.

A team try to fix their broken
_____ister in the middle of the
_____

Umbrellas

The Egyptians held umbrellas over nobles to signify the authority of those being shaded, and over members of the royalty to symbolise the 'vault of heaven' protecting them. Ancient Greeks also used the umbrella to denote their deities, but in both Greece and Rome, the device soon became more popular as a shade provider.

It took much longer for the umbrella to catch on as rain protection among Europeans than it did for them to adopt it as a sunshade. Stylish Persian traveller Jonas Hanway used his umbrella while walking through the streets of England in the mid-18th century, popularising it with men. By 1800, the umbrella coexisted with the parasol. ■

Herb of the Month

Rosemary

TRADITIONAL USES: Topical antioxidant, antibacterial, muscle and joint pain, bronchitis, circulation and memory/cognition

History Rosemary has long been a symbol of love, loyalty and remembrance, often included in ceremonies associated with both marriage and death. Sprigs of the herb were entwined into bridal wreaths or bridal bouquets. In some European countries, it is still customary for mourners to carry rosemary in funeral processions.

As a medicinal herb, rosemary has several modern-day applications. Rosemary oil is used topically to treat muscle pain and arthritis and to improve circulation. Its essential oil is employed in aromatherapy to relieve stress and anxiety. Internally, rosemary is used for indigestion, nervous tension and headaches. ■

Strange ... but True: Insects

❶ If grasshoppers were the size of people, they could leap the length of a basketball court.

❷ Dragonflies can see in all directions at once.

❸ Some ants make themselves explode when attacked.

❹ Butterflies taste food with their feet.

❺ The Asian vampire moth sometimes drinks the blood of animals.

❻ Spiders have clear blood.

❼ Ladybirds squirt smelly liquid from their knees when scared.

❽ In some places there are about as many insects in one square mile as there are people on the entire planet.

❾ Honeybees can be trained to detect explosives.

❿ Cockroaches can survive under water for up to 15 minutes.

Upside-down thrill seekers ride the Top Spin at the 176th Oktoberfest, a 16-day beer festival in Munich, Germany.

AND WHAT IS SO RARE AS A DAY IN JUNE?

JUNE

JUNE 2013

1 SATURDAY

2 SUNDAY

3 MONDAY

4 TUESDAY

5 WEDNESDAY

6 THURSDAY

7 FRIDAY

8 SATURDAY

9 SUNDAY

10 MONDAY

11 TUESDAY

12 WEDNESDAY

13 THURSDAY

14 FRIDAY

15 SATURDAY

16 SUNDAY

17 MONDAY

18 TUESDAY

19 WEDNESDAY

20 THURSDAY

21 Summer solstice
FRIDAY

22 SATURDAY

23 SUNDAY

24 MONDAY

25 TUESDAY

26 WEDNESDAY

27 THURSDAY

28 FRIDAY

29 SATURDAY

30 SUNDAY

Bird of the Month

Whitethroat
(Sylvia communis)

LENGTH: 13–15 cm

RANGE: Breeds in Europe and northern Asia; winters from Africa to India

Sylvia is related to the Latin silva 'wood, forest', and is in reference to the bird's woodland habitat. Communis, meaning 'general', derives from the Latin phrase locus communis, 'a statement generally accepted'.

Sudoku Challenge

	3		2		1		7	
7			3	4	9			2
				6				
6		9				8		3
		5				1		
4		3				2		6
				3				
5			4	7	6			1
	4		1		5		6	

Answers on p. 156

125 YEARS OF NATIONAL GEOGRAPHIC

Say 'cheese'—an oceanic whitetip shark swims past a diver.

THE UNDERWATER WORLD

Society records glow with 'firsts'—such as the 'first natural colour photographs of Arctic life' and the 'first natural colour photographs from the air'. One 'first' stands out as a true pioneering achievement. In Florida's Dry Tortugas, Charles Martin, head of the Geographic's photo lab, and ichthyologist W. H. Longley took the world's first undersea colour photographs. Martin constructed a flash-powder mechanism that was synchronised to a submerged camera encased in brass. Longley carried the camera, wearing a bulky diver's helmet with air hose attached to a compressor on a dory. On the surface, Martin tended a huge reflector and enough magnesium powder to blow up the whole project. The bursts of powder were deafening and blinding, and Longley was seriously burned. Their pictures were published in January 1927. ■

Charles Martin took the first ever underwater photos in Florida, in 1926.

June Constellation

This ancient constellation is one of the most distinct in the early summer sky. Boötes is easily identified by its brightest star, Arcturus, which is simple to find not only because it is the fourth brightest in the sky, but because it is on an arc that connects to the handle of the Plough—a reference point for the 'arc to Arcturus'.

BOÖTES

MAKEUP: 8 stars
BEST VIEWED: June
LOCATION: Summer, centre of chart
SIZE IN THE SKY: ✋
ALPHA STAR: Arcturus
DEEP SKY OBJECT: Izar, double star

Mythology Many different legends surround Boötes. According to some, he is there to keep his flock of creatures moving about the sky, as he pursues the bears, Ursa Major and Ursa Minor. In another incarnation he is the son of Callisto—the paramour of Zeus who was changed into a bear, Ursa Major, by Zeus's angered wife. He is also known as the son of Demeter, the goddess of the harvest, granted a place in the stars for inventing the plough.

About Arcturus represents the knee of Boötes. The herdsman's head is pointed towards Polaris as he runs across the night sky with one arm—upside down from a northern perspective. The Quadrantid meteor shower falls from the northern part of the constellation Boötes. One of the strongest of the year, producing several dozen meteors an hour, it takes place in the first week of January. ▪

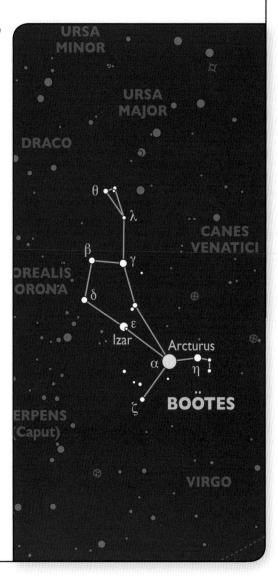

Bravest of Them All

As a fire raged in the abandoned Brooklyn garage that was her home, Scarlett the cat ran into the fire five times to rescue her kittens. Badly burned from the fire, Scarlett accounted for all of her kittens before collapsing from her injuries. By the time she was healthy again, more than 7,000 people had offered to adopt the family.

Ape Anglers

Orangutans are clearly some of the most clever animals in the world. They can saw wood, open locked doors and drink from cups. But the fiery-haired 'person of the forest' doesn't use its skills often. Instead, orangutans spend most of their time in trees, eating fruits and insects.

In Nyaru Menteng Rehabilitation Centre, Borneo, a newly released orangutan demonstrates his latest trick—stealing fish from a fisherman's rod.

So York University's Anne Russon, who studies great ape intelligence, was surprised by the new skill she observed in several formerly captive orangutans in central Indonesian Borneo: fishing. These enterprising apes—six among some three dozen now being reacquainted with the wild on a river island— use sticks to catch slower fish by hand, or simply steal lines laid by humans (left). After

examining their catch, most decide it's food. This recently observed knack for fishing is especially surprising as orangutans are particularly adept at climbing but really have no propensity for swimming.

Archaeological evidence shows that members of the *Homo* genus have been fish eaters the past two million years. Some scientists think human brain evolution depended on the fatty acids in fish and shellfish rather than on a diet of meat, and Russon says her research may support that theory. 'This indicates that the earliest hominins could have figured out how to catch fish with tools.' ■

STRANGE . . . BUT TRUE!

Some female long-tailed macaques in Thailand have been observed teaching their young how to floss (with strands of hair).

THE ENVIRONMENT

Sark Is the Night

They say on a clear day you can see forever. What about a clear night? If you're on the island of Sark, meteors, constellations and a horizon-spanning Milky Way are on view. The tiny, rustic Channel Island—2.1 square miles, 600-some residents, no cars or street lights—has long been a haven for naked-eye astronomy. In 2011, it became the first island in the world deemed a Dark Sky Place by the International Dark-Sky Association, a U.S.-based not-for-profit organisation promoting solutions to light pollution. Sark joins about a dozen places worldwide recognised by the group. Steve Owens, the astronomer who led Sark's application process, says the designation came after a six-month 'light audit' led to the retrofitting of 30 fixtures causing an orange glow. For midwinter stargazers, that means 12 hours of darkest night await. ■

The tiny island of Sark in the Channel Islands is an astronomer's paradise. The lack of light pollution means that on a clear night meteors, constellations and the Milky Way are all on view.

Simulating Wildfires

Four decades of studying fires have led Jack Cohen of the U.S. Forest Service to one conclusion: When it comes to wildfires, the greatest threat to homes isn't from walls of flame sweeping through residential areas. It's from the houses themselves—their construction, materials, even landscaping—and their susceptibility to embers, the tiny bits of burning material he calls firebrands.

Cohen has seen thousands of homes succumb to fire, including some of the approximately 5,500 consumed in the California infernos of 2003 and 2007. The following year the U.S. Department of Homeland Security agreed to fund development of software that will eventually enable homeowners and fire agencies to evaluate vulnerabilities in houses and other structures. This, says Cohen, is a vital step towards preventing disaster. To prove his point, he's enlisted an impressive tool: a full-scale house that can be set on fire, refitted with different materials and then set aflame again.

Call it playing with fire for a purpose. The simulations take place in a giant facility situated on 90 acres in the South Carolina countryside. Here the Insurance Institute for Business & Home Safety, with funding from some 60 insurance companies, re-creates the conditions of wildfires, hurricanes and the like in order to study their impact on buildings and to develop protection guidelines. 'There's nothing else like this lab,' says President and CEO Julie Rochman. 'Our number one obsession is that the science be right.'

To isolate vulnerable spots on a building in the midst of a blaze, the 1,400-square-foot test house is bombarded with embers generated by igniting bins of mulch. The structure can be fitted with different kinds of siding, windows, gutters and roofs. Among the lessons learned: vinyl gutters readily melt, and embers can infiltrate homes through vents, windows and roofs. 'We were a little surprised how quickly things happened once embers blew onto the roof,' says Rochman. 'We saw ignition in seconds.' That's the point Cohen hopes the software based on his research will drive home. 'When wildfires burn intensely, they produce millions of firebrands that come down like a blizzard,' he says. Once inside a house, they can potentially burn it from the inside out. The software will help users pinpoint areas prone to igniting. ■

Built for burning: this test house is being used in a simulation to study the effects of an ember storm typical of a wildfire.

Tasting Words and Hearing Numbers

A neural condition that tangles the senses so that people hear colours and taste words could yield important clues to understanding how the brain is organised, according to a new review study.

This sensory merger, called synaesthesia, was first scientifically documented in 1812 but was widely misunderstood for much of its history, with many experts thinking the condition was a form of mild insanity. 'It's not just that the number two is blue, but two is also a male number that wears a hat and is in love with the number seven,' said study co-author David Brang, of the University of California, San Diego (UCSD). 'We're not sure if these personifications are [also a symptom of] synaesthesia, but we think this is what derailed a lot of scientists from being interested in it … They thought these people were making it all up.'

Early misunderstandings of synaesthesia arose in part because the associations that synaesthetes described were very precise and detailed, prompting some experts at the time to link the condition with mental disorders such as schizophrenia. Today scientists have

How does that word taste to you? A condition called synaesthesia—which causes some people to hear colours or taste words—has been the subject of a new scientific study.

tools that allow them to probe the brain in ways that were impossible 200—or even 10—years ago. One such tool is a type of brain scan called DTI, short for diffusion tensor imaging, which lets scientists see the connections between different brain regions. Visualising these connections between sensory brain regions could help explain why

certain forms of synaesthesia exist and why the condition tends to be unidirectional—for example, numbers can evoke colours but colours don't typically evoke numbers.

Such studies could also help test an idea proposed by some scientists that all humans have the neural mechanism for synaesthesia but it's suppressed for some reason. Studies today also indicate that synaesthesia is about seven times more common in artists, poets and novelists than in the rest of the population, and some scientists have hypothesised that synaesthetes are better at linking unrelated ideas.

Despite recent advances, many questions about synaesthesia remain, such as whether other animals experience synaesthesia, how different brain chemicals affect the condition, and the exact role of genetics in determining a synaesthete's cognitive and creative abilities. ■

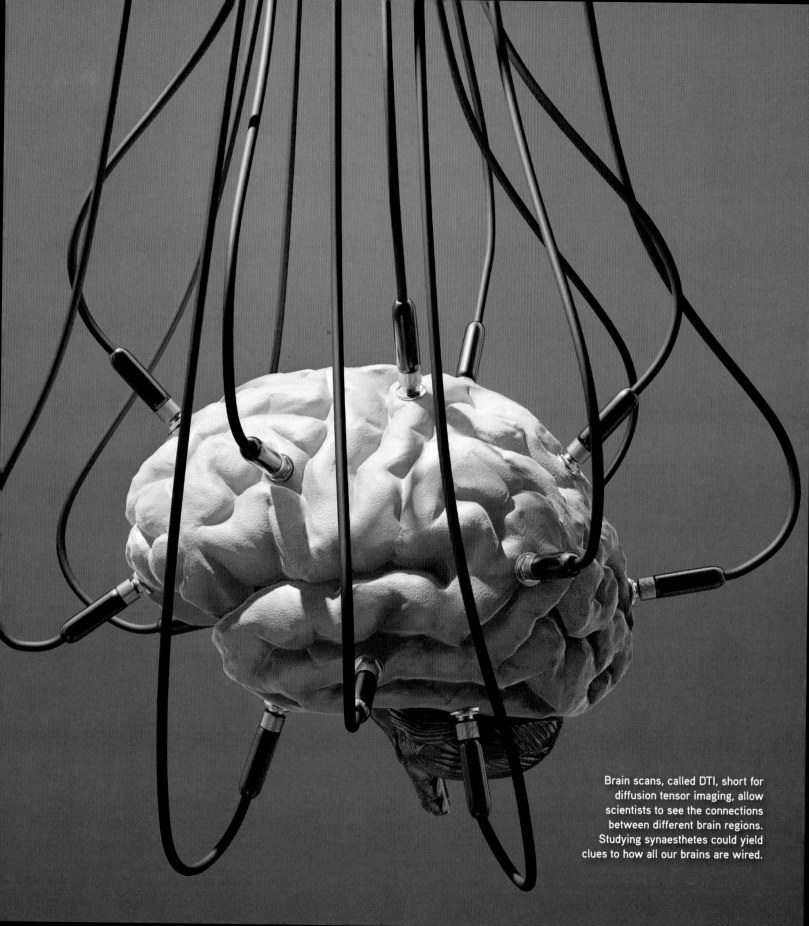

Brain scans, called DTI, short for diffusion tensor imaging, allow scientists to see the connections between different brain regions. Studying synaesthetes could yield clues to how all our brains are wired.

A clown-coloured gecko helps it-self to the leftovers of a coconut cream pie in Hawaii.

English Window Tax

A beautiful English country house with a facade full of windows might be making not an aesthetic statement but an economic one, especially if it dates from the 17th or 18th century. Many rich landowners ostentatiously added windows to demonstrate that they were able to pay the government-imposed 'window tax' that was supposed to circumvent the popular opposition to income tax. In some places in England, there are still bricked-over windows that resulted from owners who opposed or could not afford the tax, levied according to the number of windows in a home. ■

Herb of the Month

Arnica

TRADITIONAL USES: Bruises, contusions and other musculoskeletal injuries, swelling (from injuries), joint pain (from injuries or osteoarthritis)

History As the second half of its scientific name suggests, *Arnica montana* is a mountain dweller, native to sunny alpine meadows of Europe, Central Asia and Siberia. Sporting deep yellow, daisy-like flowers, arnica has been prized for its ability to ease the pain and inflammation of sore muscles, bruises and sprains. Originally the herb was used in pagan rituals designed to ensure a good harvest. Arnica blossoms, brilliant as tiny suns, were thought to be especially potent on the summer solstice. Bunches of the flowers were gathered on Midsummer Day and placed in fields to enhance the fertility of crops. ■

Strange ... but True: Travel

1 There was a hotel made of rubbish in Rome, Italy.

2 The first aeroplane journey across the United States took 49 days.

3 The first space tourist paid $20 million for a ten-day trip to the International Space Station.

4 A Russian man drove a tractor more than 12,986 miles in 19 days—that's longer than the distance from London to Los Angeles, U.S.A.

5 A traffic jam in China lasted for more than a week.

6 Rockets must travel at least 25,000 miles per hour to escape Earth's gravity.

7 More than two million animals fly in aeroplanes every year.

8 The world's first underwater hotel is in Key Largo, Florida.

A caiman hunts in a seasonal river known as Vazante do Castelo at the end of the wet season in Fazenda Barra Mansa, Brazil.

A SWARM OF BEES IN JULY IS NOT WORTH A FLY

JULY

JULY 2013

1 MONDAY

2 TUESDAY

3 WEDNESDAY

4 THURSDAY

5 FRIDAY

6 SATURDAY

7 SUNDAY

8 MONDAY

9 TUESDAY

10 WEDNESDAY

11 THURSDAY

12 FRIDAY

13 SATURDAY

14 SUNDAY

15 MONDAY

16 TUESDAY

17 WEDNESDAY

18 THURSDAY

19 FRIDAY

20 SATURDAY

21 SUNDAY

22 MONDAY

23 TUESDAY

24 WEDNESDAY

25 THURSDAY

26 FRIDAY

27 SATURDAY

28 SUNDAY

29 MONDAY

30 TUESDAY

31 WEDNESDAY

Bird of the Month

Bee-eater *(Merops apiaster)*

LENGTH: 25–29 cm
RANGE: Breeds from southern Europe to Afghanistan; winters in tropical Africa

Merops is related to Merope, one of the seven Pleiades, daughter of the Titan Atlas. Her name has been interpreted to mean 'with sparkling face', and could refer to the bird's bright colours. Apiaster comes from the Latin apis, meaning 'bee'.

GEO PUZZLE

Sudoku Challenge

3	2		8		4		5	7
		9		7				
7								4
	5	7		9	4			
	7						6	
	4	3		6	5			
6	3							3
		4		8				
5	4		6		2		1	9

Answers on p. 156

125 YEARS OF NATIONAL GEOGRAPHIC

White-tailed deer trip a wire connected to a camera in one of the first ever nighttime shots published by *National Geographic* magazine in 1906.

FIRST WILDLIFE PHOTOS PUBLISHED

In July 1906, the Editor-in-Chief of *National Geographic* magazine, Gilbert H. Grosvenor, devoted an entire issue to wildlife: 'Photographing Wild Game with Flashlight and Camera', written and shot by George Shiras III, a former U.S. congressman who hunted with a camera. Seventy-four candid photographs captured animals—deer, porcupines and a lynx—as they tripped across triggers in the darkness. Shiras's photos caused a sensation. President Theodore Roosevelt was enthralled, and letters poured in from readers demanding more natural history. The issue's popularity helped confirm Grosvenor's faith in the editorial value of photography. ■

The first published wildlife photographs were met with a huge public response.

July Constellation

Scorpius is one of the most evocative images in the night sky. Two of the twenty-five brightest stars in the sky are in this constellation. For northern observers, it is best spotted in the summertime towards the south along the Milky Way, between zodiac partners Sagittarius and Libra.

SCORPIUS

MAKEUP: 17 stars

BEST VIEWED: Jul/Aug

LOCATION: Summer, southwest quadrant

SIZE IN THE SKY: ✋

ALPHA STAR: Antares

DEEP SKY OBJECT: M6, Butterfly cluster

Mythology This celestial shape has been significant to many civilizations. Chinese astronomers saw a mighty dragon. Ancient Greek mythology recognises Scorpius as the animal that defeated the hunter Orion; he was able to inflict the fatal wound on the hero's leg, which is now visible in the sky. The hunter and scorpion are on opposite sides of the heavens to keep them separated, with Scorpius rising in the east in the spring just as Orion sets in the west after a winter in the northern sky.

About Unlike many constellations, Scorpius very much resembles its namesake animal, from its wide, pincer-armed head to a torso and a twisted tail that ends with the bright star Shaula. For novice star watchers, Scorpius is among the easier constellations to recognise, both because of its shape and because of the 1st-magnitude star, Antares, that sits at its heart. ■

Ancient Popcorn Found

A new study says that people in what's now Peru were eating the snack 2,000 years earlier than thought. Coastal peoples were preparing corn-based foods up to 6,700 years ago, according to analysis of ancient corn-cobs, husks and stalks recently unearthed at the archaeological sites on Peru's northern coast.

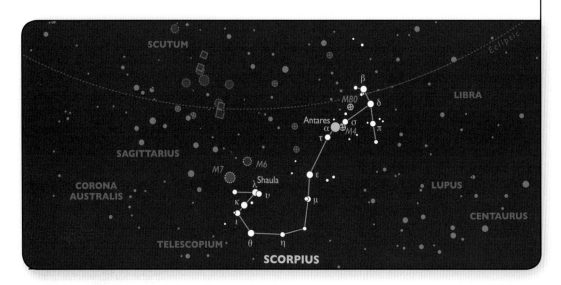

Fish Mimics Mimic Octopus That Mimics Fish

The mimic octopus can take on the forms of a lionfish, a jellyfish, a shrimp, a crab and more than ten other animals. But now a jawfish in Indonesia has been seen one-upping the marine master of disguise—it mimics the mimic octopus.

Researcher Godehard Kopp was diving off South Sulawesi Province when he noticed a tiny yellow-and-black striped jawfish swimming alongside a similarly coloured mimic octopus. Surprised, Kopp, of the University of Göttingen in Germany, filmed the event and sent the video to biologists Luiz Rocha and Rich Ross at the California Academy of Sciences for their interpretation. Rocha and Ross only compounded the mystery. 'We've never seen anything like that before,' Rocha said.

Jawfish normally stay hidden in ocean burrows, avoiding predators. 'I've never seen one swimming in the open,' Rocha said. Not only was it out in the open, but the jawfish was wiggling its body 'almost like a tentacle', and closely followed the mimic

The highest form of flattery? A jawfish was recently spotted imitating a mimic octopus, a type of octopus itself known for pretending to be other animals, including a lionfish, jellyfish or crab.

octopus for at least a quarter of an hour.

The fish probably stuck close to the octopus—which didn't seem to notice its 'hitchhiker'—to take advantage of the camouflage while looking for food or a new burrow. They're not sure whether the event is a one-off or if the jawfish 'does that every time' an octopus comes by.

The jawfish's species is also in question. It looks like a black-marble jawfish, but because this is the first time a jawfish has been documented performing any kind of mimicry, Rocha said, he has to wonder if there's some chance the Indonesian fish might be genetically distinct from its far-flung cousins. ■

STRANGE . . . BUT TRUE!

Some species of fish can change from female to male.

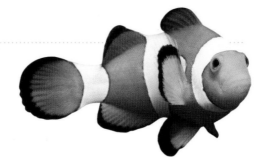

Geography Q&A

Q 1 Which British county is the home of Cheddar cheese?

Q 2 Which country moved its capital from Istanbul to the more centrally located Ankara in the early 20th century?

← **Q 3** To visit the home of the famous painter Rubens and to walk through the world's largest diamond district in Antwerp, you would travel to which country?

Answers on p. 155

PALAEONTOLOGY

Jurassic Mother Lode

Pterosaurs died out with the dinosaurs, leaving more mysteries than fossils. Now palaeontologists who study the flying vertebrates are starting to make headway. In 2009 a transitional form in pterosaur evolution, Darwinopterus, was found in China. The dig site yielded a 160-million-year-old fossil of one with an egg. The University of Leicester's David Unwin says the egg bolsters the hypothesis that pterosaurs were sexually distinct: females had wider hips, and only males had head crests. Other experts agree, but Kevin Padian of the University of California, Berkeley, argues that we don't yet know enough about pterosaur maturation to say whether age or gender accounts for physical differences among fossils. More scrutiny may resolve the uncertainty. ■

A 160-million-year-old fossil reveals a pterosaur with an egg, shedding some light on the mysterious dinosaur.

Drilling to the Mantle

Deep within the Earth lies lustrous green rock that holds the key to mysteries about the origins of our planet. It's part of a layer—the mantle—that makes up 84 per cent of the Earth's volume. Bits of the rock, modified by heat and pressure, are spit from volcanoes and prized in polished form as the gem peridot. But no one has ever laid eyes on fresh mantle peridotite. Now an international team aims to bore through the Earth's crust to retrieve the first sample. 'Pristine mantle would be a geochemical treasure trove equivalent to the Apollo lunar rocks,' says the University of Southampton's Damon Teagle. Scientists are scouting spots off Costa Rica, Baja California and Hawaii for the best site to drill. There sediments are thin and the mantle is cool enough to core. But the seafloor is some 2.5 miles down, making drilling operations deep even by oil industry standards. Reaching the target distance is now feasible with the Japanese ship *Chikyu,* which can hold more than six miles of drill pipes. And drill bits with tungsten carbide teeth are being refined to tackle ultra-hard rocks that have ruined equipment in previous attempts. The big dig is set to start before the decade's end. ■

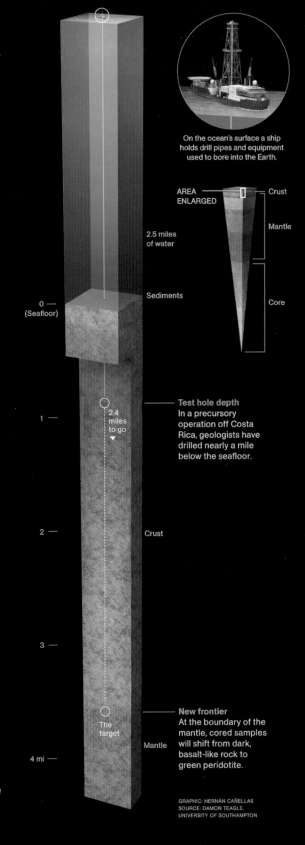

On the ocean's surface a ship holds drill pipes and equipment used to bore into the Earth.

AREA ENLARGED

Crust

Mantle

Core

2.5 miles of water

0 — (Seafloor)

Sediments

1 —

2.4 miles to go ▼

Test hole depth
In a precursory operation off Costa Rica, geologists have drilled nearly a mile below the seafloor.

2 —

Crust

3 —

The target

New frontier
At the boundary of the mantle, cored samples will shift from dark, basalt-like rock to green peridotite.

Mantle

4 mi —

GRAPHIC: HERNÁN CAÑELLAS
SOURCE: DAMON TEAGLE, UNIVERSITY OF SOUTHAMPTON

This diagram shows the challenge facing scientists hoping to drill into the Earth's mantle. The gem peridot (inset) is a piece of mantle modified by heat and pressure and brought to the surface by a volcano.

Secrets of Panda Poo Revealed

A new analysis of panda poo has finally answered an age-old question: how do giant pandas survive on a diet that's 99 per cent bamboo when they have the guts of carnivores?

Plant-eating animals tend to have longer intestines to aid in digesting fibrous material, a trait the black-and-white bears lack. What's more, when the giant panda's genome was sequenced in 2009, scientists found that the creature lacks the genes for any known enzymes that would help break down cellulose, the plant fibres found in bamboo and other grasses. This led researchers to speculate that panda intestines must have cellulose-munching bacteria that play a role in digestion. But previous attempts to find such bacteria in panda guts had failed.

The new study looked at gene sequences in the droppings from seven wild and eight captive giant pandas—a much bigger sample than was used in previous panda-poo studies, said study leader Fuwen Wei, of the Chinese Academy of Science's Institute of Zoology in Beijing. Wei and colleagues found that pandas' digestive tracts do in fact

Bamboo and other grasses are made from the plant fibre cellulose—but without the enzymes to break it down it's very difficult to derive any nutrients from the plant.

contain bacteria similar to those in the intestines of herbivores.

Thirteen of the bacteria species that the team identified are from a family known to break down cellulose, but seven of those species are unique to pandas. 'We think this may be caused by different diet, the unique inner habitat of the gut, or the unique phylogenetic

position of their host', since pandas are on a different branch of the tree of life than most herbivores, Wei said.

Even with help from bacteria in their gut, pandas don't derive much nutrition from bamboo—a panda digests just 17 per cent of the 9 to 14 kilograms of dry food it eats each day. This explains why pandas also evolved a sluggish, energy-conserving lifestyle.

So how and why did pandas become plant-eaters in the first place? Some scientists theorise that, as the ancient human population increased, pandas were pushed into higher altitudes. The animals then adopted a bamboo diet so they wouldn't compete for prey with other meat-eaters, such as Asiatic black bears, in their new homes, said Nicole MacCorkle, a panda keeper at the Smithsonian's National Zoo in Washington, D.C. Pandas will eat meat if it's offered to them, MacCorkle added, but they won't actively hunt for it. ∎

So why are pandas herbivores if their digestive system isn't suited to this diet? Some scientists think that pandas started to eat bamboo when forced to move to higher altitudes by an expanding human population.

It's a dog's day at a local beach
where bikini-clad bathers gather.

Bathtub Gin

The classic 'long drink', gin and tonic is also known as G&T or gin and it, depending on the country, social station and drinking venue. It may also be the only cocktail that was concocted for a medicinal purpose. British troops who were stationed in hot, damp climates during the 19th century were prone to suffering from bouts of malaria, and tonic water made with Peruvian quinine was found to be the best anti-malarial substance. However, quinine (extracted from the bark of the cinchona tree) was quite bitter, and some enterprising officers found that if you mixed it with gin, sugar and some lime juice, the tonic water was quite palatable and refreshing. ■

NATURAL HEALING

Herb of the Month

Hops

TRADITIONAL USES: Digestion, nervousness, insomnia and menopause

History The Roman physician Pliny the Elder named hops *Lupus salictarius*, which means 'willow wolf' and refers to the vine's habit of twining around other plants and strangling them, like a wolf does to sheep. The plant's species name, *lupulus*, is Latin for 'small wolf'. Hops were used medicinally in Europe and by Native Americans in North America.

In modern herbal medicine, hops are valued for their soothing, sedative effect. Tea made from hops is good for calming nervous tension. The bitter flavour of hops is thought to help strengthen and stimulate digestion, and may ease muscle spasms in the digestive tract associated with irritable bowel syndrome. ■

PUB TRIVIA

Strange ... but True: People

1. A woman hand-delivered a pizza from London, England, to Melbourne, Australia—a distance of about 10,350 miles.

2. Your fingernails take six months to grow from base to tip.

3. Koalas and humans have similar fingerprints.

4. Your eyes move about 80 times a second.

5. Humans can recognise about 10,000 different smells.

6. If about 33 million people held hands, they could make a circle around the Equator.

7. A New York man did a continuous series of somersaults for 21 miles.

8. A person once hiccupped for 68 years.

9. A man was struck by lightning seven times and lived.

A reveller slides headlong through a sea of tomato juice in Buñol, southern Spain, as part of La Tomatina festival. The one-hour food fight can use up to 276,000 pounds (125,000 kilograms) of tomatoes.

DRY AUGUST AND WARM DOTH HARVEST NO HARM

UGUST

AUGUST 2013

1 THURSDAY

2 FRIDAY

3 SATURDAY

4 SUNDAY

5 MONDAY

6 TUESDAY ●

7 WEDNESDAY

8 THURSDAY

9 FRIDAY

10 SATURDAY

11 SUNDAY

12 MONDAY

13 TUESDAY

14 WEDNESDAY ◐

15 THURSDAY

16 FRIDAY

17 SATURDAY

18 SUNDAY

19 MONDAY

20 TUESDAY ○

21 WEDNESDAY

22 THURSDAY

23 FRIDAY

24 SATURDAY

25 SUNDAY

26 Summer Bank Holiday
MONDAY

27 TUESDAY

28 WEDNESDAY ◑

29 THURSDAY

30 FRIDAY

31 SATURDAY

Bird of the Month

Swallow *(Hirundo rustica)*

LENGTH: 17–21 cm
RANGE: Almost worldwide,
known as Barn Swallow in the U.S.

The word swallow has uncertain origins. It is related to Germanic forms such as the Middle High German swalwe and the Middle English swalowe (from the Old English swalwe). It may also be related to the Slavic words for nightingale, such as the Polish słowik.

Sudoku Challenge

6			1		8			9
	5	8	9		2	4	1	
1			5		7			2
	7					2		
	1						8	
	6					5		
5			6		3			8
	6	3	8		9	1	7	
8			4		1			3

Answers on p. 156

125 YEARS OF NATIONAL GEOGRAPHIC

Previous to *Explorer II* Capts. Orvil Anderson and Albert W. Stevens narrowly escaped disaster aboard *Explorer I* in 1934.

DEEP SEAS, HIGH SKIES

The June 1931 *National Geographic* published William Beebe's account of climbing with Otis Barton into a steel bathysphere off Bermuda and plunging deeper into the ocean than any person before them. In 1934, under Geographic sponsorship, Beebe and Barton descended nearly twice as deep, to 923 metres, a depth record that stood for the next 15 years.

William Beebe emerges from the bathysphere used in the 1934 dive.

The March 1933 *National Geographic* carried the accounts of balloonist Auguste Piccard's record-breaking ascents to altitudes of more than 10 miles, in hydrogen-filled balloons. 'The stratosphere is the superhighway of future intercontinental transport,' Piccard predicted. In 1935 National Geographic Society joined the U.S. Army Air Corps to sponsor the *Explorer II*, which set a balloon altitude record of 22,065 metres that stood for the next 21 years. ■

August Constellation

Aquila (Latin for 'eagle'), named by star gazers in ancient Mesopotamia, flies close enough to the Earth's Equator to be seen from anywhere in the world. But it is most easily found in the northern hemisphere when looking south in the middle of the summer months.

AQUILA

MAKEUP: 10 stars
BEST VIEWED: Aug/Sept
LOCATION: Summer, southeast quadrant
SIZE IN THE SKY: ✋
ALPHA STAR: Altair
DEEP SKY OBJECT: Eta Aquilae, variable star

Mythology The eagle belonged to the Greek god Zeus and, according to myth, carried the god's thunderbolts for him. He was also said to have brought to the sky a young shepherd named Ganymede who was to serve as Zeus's cupbearer. The youth would be immortalised as the nearby constellation Aquarius. Aquila has been visualised as flying in two different directions.

About Altair (Arabic for 'the bird') is the constellation's brightest star and represents the eagle's head. It is also part of the trio of stars that forms the Summer Triangle asterism, and as one of the brightest stars in the sky makes a good reference point for identifying the constellation. The supergiant Eta Aquilae is another notable feature in the constellation. It is a variable star that ranges from magnitude 4.1 to 5.3 every 7.2 days. ■

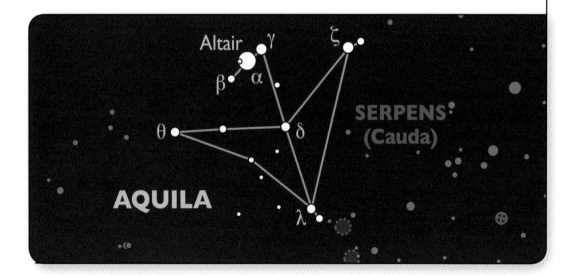

Altair γ ζ
β α
θ δ **SERPENS (Cauda)**
AQUILA
λ

Celestial Bloom

Hubble Space Telescope recently focused the instrument on a pair of galaxies known as Arp 273, which had spun themselves into something surreally terrestrial: a rose. The above interaction occurred a few hundred million years ago, as the lower galaxy (UGC 1813) dived through the outside arms of the upper one (UGC 1810).

Toxic Nudi-whats?

Bright blues, proud purples, garish greens—the colours of seabound nudibranchs (better known as sea slugs) are beautiful to the eye but deadly to the touch. Their stunning colours are some of their best known characteristics, but are toxic and are derived from the food they eat.

The remarkable colours displayed by this pair of *Nembrotha kubaryana* nudibranchs are not just for show; they warn predators of the nudibranchs' powerful toxicity.

Nudibranchs have nothing between their skin and the ocean—no protective shells or pointy spikes—to keep predators at bay. But their bold colour scheme actually serves as a first line of defence; in the wild, a bright palette is often an indication of toxicity, so hunters often keep their distance from the colourful nudibranch, which means 'naked gill'.

There are 3,000 different species of nudibranch, united by a defence system that rivals the Marines'. Although they don't have the hard shells of other molluscs, their arsenal includes toxic secretions and stinging cells. Some make their own poisons, but others borrow from the food they eat, dining on toxic sponges, for instance, and then storing the irritating compounds to be released when they become agitated. Other nudibranchs ingest fire corals and anemones, to which they are immune, later letting those poisons loose.

This makes them less than appetising on the plate, although sea spiders, turtles and a few crabs can stomach them. Some people consume them, but only after removing the toxic organs. If nothing else, it must be acknowledged: this sea slug appears a worthy adversary. ■

STRANGE ... BUT TRUE!

Some slugs have 3,000 teeth and 'only' 4 noses.

Geography Q & A

Q ① What theory explains the shifting positions and ongoing movements of the continents?

← **Q** ② What is the term for an area of desert where an underground water source supports vegetation growth?

Q ③ What Norwegian word is used for a narrow, steep-sided inlet of the sea that was carved by a glacier?

Answers on p. 155

PALAEONTOLOGY

Prehistoric Easy Glider

While hunting for shark's teeth in Chile a few years ago, fossil collectors hit a giant jackpot: the nearly intact remains of a prehistoric seabird whose wingspan stretched over five metres. 'It's one of the largest ever recorded for a living or extinct bird,' says David Rubilar-Rogers, co-author of a 2010 study on the specimen. Called *Pelagornis chilensis,* the species lived roughly seven million years ago and had a beak full of spiky bone protrusions resembling teeth—likely used for snatching slippery ocean prey. At 70 per cent complete, the fossil is a rare find, as birds from the same family had bones that were easily crushed. Could birds any bigger have flown? An answer could be waiting in the wings. ■

WINGSPANS

Pigeon 0.6 m

Bald eagle 2 m

Albatross 3.5 m

Pelagornis chilensis 5 m

This diagram shows the enormous 17-foot (5-metre) wingspan of prehistoric seabird *Pelagornis chilensis* in relation to some of our modern birds.

Male Spiders Give 'Back Rubs' to Seduce Their Mates

For many spiders, females of the species are much bigger than the males—*N. pilipes* females are up to ten times larger—so mating is always a risky proposition. An unlucky suitor might get interrupted in his carnal embrace when a female kicks him off and eats him.

Male spiders have evolved multiple techniques to avoid this fate, at least before finishing the deed. Male black widows, for instance, pick up scents from females that help the males determine how hungry their love interests are before attempting to mate. Redback spiders in Australia, meanwhile, actually allow themselves to be snacked on to prolong their time with a female.

A male golden orb-weaver's (*Nephila pilipes's*) strategy involves another trait common among spiders: pedipalps, a pair of appendages that includes male genitals, said study co-author Matjaz Kuntner, of the Smithsonian's National Museum of Natural History and the Slovenian Academy of Sciences and Arts.

The male's pedipalps fit perfectly into the female's two genital openings, and he can leave them behind to 'plug' the openings. But a male needs to mate several times in succession to plug both openings and guarantee the female—which can have multiple partners—will have his offspring. To make his mate more receptive in between bouts, a male *N. pilipes* will spread silk over her dorsum, or back, in massage-like motions known as mate binding. ■

She's the boss! The large difference in size between the male (top) and female golden orb-weaver spiders makes it tricky for the male to mate effectively without being eaten.

A Deadly Prehistoric Tryst

Neanderthals may have been victims of love, or at least of interspecies breeding, according to a new study. Venturing farther and farther to cope with climate change, they increasingly mated with our own species, giving rise to mixed-species humans.

Over generations of genetic mixing, the Neanderthal genome would have dissolved, absorbed into the *Homo sapiens* population, which was much larger. 'If you increase the mobility of the groups in the places where they live, you end up increasing the gene flow between the two different populations, until eventually one population disappears as a clearly defined group,' said C. Michael Barton, an archaeologist at Arizona State University's School of Human Evolution and Social Change.

Some theories suggest Neanderthals disappeared about 30,000 years ago because the species wasn't able to adapt to a cooling world as well as *Homo sapiens*.

Barton tells a different tale, suggesting that Neanderthals reacted to the onset of the Ice Age in the same ways modern humans did—by ranging farther for food and other resources. 'As glaciation increased, there was likely less

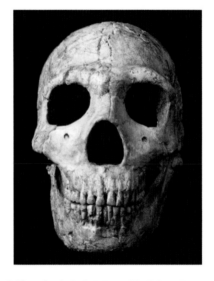

A Neanderthal skull from Wadi Amud, a stream in the Upper Galilee. Neanderthals were a relation of early humans, but no one knows for sure what caused them to die out 30,000 years ago.

diversity in land use, so Neanderthals and modern humans alike focused on a particular survival strategy that we still see today at high latitudes,' Barton said.

'They establish a home base and send out foraging parties to bring back resources. People move farther and have more opportunity to come into contact with other groups at greater distances. The archaeological record suggests that this became more and more common in Eurasia as we move toward full glaciation.' More frequent contact led to more frequent mating, the theory goes, as the two groups were forced to share the same dwindling resources. 'Other things might have happened,' Barton said. 'But in science we try to find the simplest explanation for things. This theory doesn't include massive migrations or invasions—just people doing what they normally do.'

To estimate the effects of the assumed rise in interspecies mating, Barton's team conducted a computational modelling study that spanned 1,500 Neanderthal generations. In the end, the model results supported the idea that Neanderthals were 'genetically swamped' by modern humans. ∎

Pictured here is the first reconstruction of a Neanderthal created using evidence from fossil anatomy and ancient DNA. Scientists have nicknamed her 'Wilma'.

The famous sail-shaped Burj Al Arab hotel in Dubai casts a green glow over the Persian Gulf, as jagged darts of lightning illuminate the sky behind.

Chocolate

First harvested and used by the ancient Maya, chocolate was initially a beverage, and not a particularly sweet or smooth one. The bitter blend of ground cacao beans, water and other local ingredients (including chillies, pimento and vanilla) was tough to swallow.

The first chocolate bar was introduced in 1847 by Joseph Fry & Sons in Bristol, England, and a few years later the public was introduced to enrobed chocolates at Britain's Great Exhibition of 1851. Boxed chocolates were sold in both England and America, and first marketed to the masses in 1868, with John Cadbury's packaged creams and bonbons. ∎

Herb of the Month

Aloe

TRADITIONAL USES: Burns (first and second degree), psoriasis, colitis, diabetes

History In ancient Egypt, aloe was known as the plant of immortality. Legend has it that Cleopatra massaged aloe gel into her skin as part of her daily beauty routine. Greek philosopher Aristotle is said to have urged his student Alexander the Great to claim a group of islands off the Horn of Africa to acquire the aloes that grew there for his army's medicinal arsenal. Aloe found its way into European herbal medicine by the tenth century. The gel was applied externally to soothe and heal wounds and maintain healthy skin. Internally, herbalists prescribed it for stomach disorders, insomnia, haemorrhoids, headaches, gum diseases and kidney ailments. ∎

Strange ... but True: Colour

❶ Seeing the colour red can make your heart beat faster.

❷ It is impossible to see a full rainbow in the sky at midday.

❸ More men are colour-blind than women.

❹ A river in Canada once turned red.

❺ Studies show that painting your room blue could make you more creative.

❻ Chromophobia is the extreme fear of colours.

❼ Red diamonds are some of the rarest stones in the world.

❽ Bees can be green, blue or red.

❾ Rainbow-coloured grasshoppers live in the rain forests of Peru.

❿ Cold stars are red. Hot stars are blue.

SEPT

Novices at the Dechen Phodrang monastic school in Thimphu, Bhutan, race downhill to the dining hall.

DEPARTING SUMMER HATH ASSUMED

EMBER

SEPTEMBER 2013

1 SUNDAY

2 MONDAY

3 TUESDAY

4 WEDNESDAY

5 THURSDAY

6 FRIDAY

7 SATURDAY

8 SUNDAY

9 MONDAY

10 TUESDAY

11 WEDNESDAY

12 THURSDAY

13 FRIDAY

14 SATURDAY

15 SUNDAY

16 MONDAY

17 TUESDAY

18 WEDNESDAY

19 THURSDAY

20 FRIDAY

21 SATURDAY

22 SUNDAY

23 MONDAY

24 TUESDAY

25 WEDNESDAY

26 THURSDAY

27 FRIDAY

28 SATURDAY

29 SUNDAY

30 MONDAY

Bird of the Month

Northern Wheatear

(Oenanthe oenanthe)

LENGTH: 14.5–16 cm

RANGE: Breeds in the northern hemisphere, winters primarily in Africa.

Oenanthe is Greek for vine (oine) blossom (anthos). Aristotle first mentioned the bird by this name, which might have been due to the fact that the bird migrated to the area during the blossoming of the vines.

Sudoku Challenge

	6				7			
	5		6		2			
4	7	8		9		5	6	1
6			7		9			2
3			4		2			8
9	1	7		2		8	5	6
		2		7		9		
		3				4		

Answers on p. 156

A brightly dressed person used against a beautiful landscape showcases the capabilities of Kodachrome. By the 1950s, when this image was taken in Belgium, the technique had been playfully nicknamed the 'red shirt' school of photography.

KODACHROME REVOLUTIONISED THE MAGAZINE

In the 1930s 'miniature' 35mm cameras paired with a dazzling new colour film, Kodachrome, to revolutionise the magazine. Luis Marden, a self-educated, multilingual colour enthusiast, arrived at *National Geographic* magazine in 1934. He immediately saw the potential in the new combina-

An example of a 35mm camera, which used a dazzling new colour film, Kodachrome

tion. Kodachrome offered the richest colour yet, it could be enlarged easily, and its enhanced speed allowed photographers to shoot with small 35mm cameras. No more tripods and posed pictures; no more glass plates packed into steamer trunks. Action pictures in colour were possible for the first time. Melville Grosvenor remembered the heady intoxication: 'We just threw out our other pictures from the field, just scrapped them and replaced them as fast as we could with Kodachromes. I'll never forget that—that was really a thrill.' ■

September Constellation

This southern constellation—low to the horizon even at its highest for northern mid-latitude observers—still has the advantage of being marked by Fomalhaut, a 1st-magnitude star lying in a relatively dim section of sky. Fomalhaut is a relatively young star, between 100 million and 300 million years old.

PISCIS AUSTRINUS

MAKEUP: 11 stars
BEST VIEWED: Sep/Oct
LOCATION: Autumn, southwest quadrant
SIZE IN THE SKY: 🖐🖐
ALPHA STAR: Fomalhaut
DEEP SKY OBJECT: None

Mythology Piscis Austrinus is one of the original 48 constellations identified by Ptolemy. Early artwork of this constellation depicts the sea creature with an open mouth, drinking water poured from the jug of Aquarius. The ancient Egyptians saw this group of stars as a fish; indeed the name Fomalhaut is derived from the Arabic translation for 'mouth of the fish'. One Assyrian story suggests that the fish represents the creature Oannes, who was a teacher during the day but transformed at night.

About Piscis Austrinus is easily identified in the autumn just south of Aquarius and east of Capricornus, its companions in this 'watery' section of the sky. Fomalhaut is the most distinct object in this constellation, the 18th brightest star to the naked eye, and just 25 light-years from Earth. ■

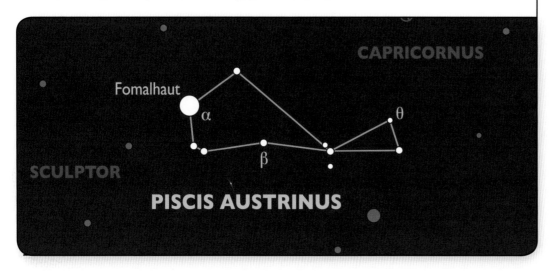

CAPRICORNUS

Fomalhaut

α

θ

β

SCULPTOR

PISCIS AUSTRINUS

Wicked Beauty

Curses, convulsions, poisonous peashooters—some plants inspire poetry, some evoke the dark arts. 'Most people are amazed that so many common plants have toxins and can kill you,' says Trevor Jones, who tends an educational 'poison garden' near Alnwick Castle, Northumberland. Adding to this menace, there are some species thought to have medicinal properties that are toxic.

New 'Giant' Lizard Discovery

A human-size lizard has hid from science high in the trees. It has a double penis, is as long as a tall human and lives in a heavily populated area of the Philippines. Yet somehow the highly secretive, giant lizard *Varanus bitatawa* has gone undetected by science on the populated island of Luzon until now.

Long known to Filipino tribal hunters, the monitor lizard was identified as a new species in 2009 via its DNA, scale pattern, size and peculiar penis, a new study says. At about two metres long, the new lizard species is closely related to the world's largest living lizard, the Komodo dragon. Unlike the Komodo, *Varanus bitatawa* has evolved to be a vegetarian. These fruit-eating lizards are also 'incredibly secretive', said study team member and biologist Daniel Bennett of Mampam Conservation. 'You could stay in that forest for years and have absolutely no idea that they are there,' Bennett said. 'They spend all their time high up in trees, more than 20 metres above the ground.'

The team captured specimens of both *V. bitatawa* and the extremely rare but

Despite its size, scientists were unaware of the existence of the giant lizard *Varanus bitatawa* on Luzon island in the Philippines until recently.

closely related Gray's monitor lizard (*Varanus olivaceus*). Capturing both types of lizard allowed the team to inspect the two

monitor lizards side by side and detect subtle differences that can help determine whether the animals represent different species.

One particularly revealing trait was the double-ended penis common to monitor lizards. The shape of this reptilian feature is unique to each species. The giant-lizard find 'adds to the recognition of the Philippines as a global conservation hot spot and a regional superpower of biodiversity,' the study team says. ∎

STRANGE ...BUT TRUE!

The smallest monkey in the world lives in South America and is about as tall as a toothbrush.

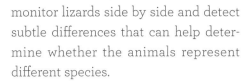

Geography Q&A

Q 1 Scientists believe that about 120 million years ago, South America began to break away from which other continent?

Q 2 The world's longest coral reef is in the Pacific Ocean off the northeast coast of which continent?

Q 3 Which continent produces the largest total amount of rice?

Answers on p. 155

PHYSICS

Shake It Off

It all begins with a twist of the head—one so powerful it leads to full-body, high-speed oscillations that whip water in all directions. Although hazardous to nearby humans, the wet-dog shake is an elegant, effective drying mechanism, says Andrew Dickerson, an engineering student at Georgia Institute of Technology who analysed the mechanics of this everyday canine act.

In taking less than a second to disperse half the water in a hound's fur, the motion is 'more efficient than a washing machine's spin cycle,' he says. Using slow-motion video, Dickerson also measured rates of oscillation in other animals and found that the smaller they are, the faster they shake. Being wet adds weight, notes veterinarian Nicholas Dodman, and that makes it harder to run. ■

Nearby humans beware! A Labrador demonstrates this incredibly efficient method of drying off wet fur.

Bible Accounts Supported by Dead Sea Disaster Record

Sediment cores from the Dead Sea reveal that the body of water may once have completely dried up, researchers say. The discovery raises fears the sea could vanish again. The same cores also show records of droughts and earthquakes that could be interpreted as supporting accounts in the Bible.

The salty sea—actually a lake—whose surface now lies more than 420 metres below sea level, is not only the lowest nonmarine place on Earth but also the catchment basin for water flowing from much of Jordan, Israel, Syria, Lebanon and Palestine. Drilling cores collected in 2010 revealed clear annual layers, almost like tree rings, said geologist Steven Goldstein of Columbia University's Lamont-Doherty Earth Observatory.

The team also found 'jumbled' sections in the Dead Sea sediment, where normally rhythmic layers had been stirred together by large earthquakes, Goldstein said. 'What I can tell you,' he said, 'is that there are a lot of earthquake deposits throughout the core', which stretches back about 200,000 years.

Looking further back, one of the seismically active eras revealed by the core samples appears to have been about 4,000 years ago. 'If you believe the biblical chronology, this is roughly [the time of] Sodom and Gomorrah,' he said. During this period, according to the Book of Genesis, God 'rained fire and brimstone from heaven, and destroyed all'. ■

Research into the layers of sediment at the bottom of the Dead Sea reveals evidence of huge seismic disruptions at various points in 200,000 years of its history.

Ordering for Seven Billion

Here's an uncomfortable maths problem: By 2045 Earth's population will likely have swelled from seven to nine billion people. To fill all those stomachs—while accounting for shifting consumption patterns, climate change and a finite amount of arable land and potable water—some experts say global food production will have to double. How can we make the numbers add up?

Julian Cribb, author of *The Coming Famine,* says higher yielding crop varieties and more efficient farming methods will be crucial. So will waste reduction. Cribb and other experts urge cities to reclaim nutrients and water from waste streams and preserve farmland. Poor countries, they say, can improve crop storage and packaging. And rich nations could cut back on resource-intensive foods like meat.

In fact, wherever easy access to cheap food means people buy more than they consume, we could all start by shopping smarter—and clearing our plates. As Cribb notes, food security is increasingly a collective challenge. It's also a chance 'to pull together on

Increased agricultural research into crop productivity is important to meeting the coming challenge of food security.

something we can all agree about, share and enjoy'.

What are some of the ways we can rise to the challenge of food security?

Adjust Diets: Less meat can mean more food. Soya beans, for instance, provide up to 15 times more protein per acre than land set aside for meat production, according to the National Soya Bean Research Laboratory.

Increase Research: Global grain yields aren't increasing fast enough, and scientists warn that a fungus could potentially imperil commercial wheat. Yet in recent decades, agricultural research and development has become less focused on productivity.

Reduce Waste: Up to half the world's harvest disappears 'between field and fork', says the Stockholm International Water Institute. Waste, diversion to animal feed and consumer behaviour all play a role. ■

Availability of arable land for growing crops is finite, but somehow we will have to produce enough food for the seven to nine billion people who are predicted to make up Earth's population by 2045.

Waste not, want not

This meal shows the average amount of food purchased, and wasted, per person in the United States during the course of a year.*

Purchased 35 kg — Wasted 10 kg

Fresh fruit

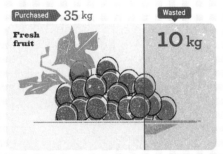

60 kg — **18 kg** WASTED

Fresh vegetables

76 kg — 15 kg WASTED

Milk

2 kg — 0.3 kg WASTED

Butter

32 kg — **12 kg** WASTED

Poultry

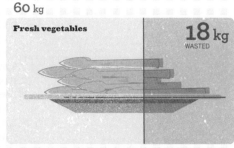

78 kg — 16 kg WASTED

Grain products

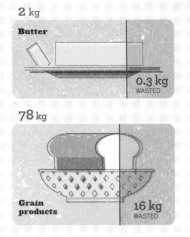

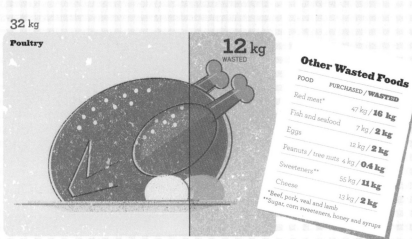

Other Wasted Foods

FOOD	PURCHASED / **WASTED**
Red meat*	47 kg / **16 kg**
Fish and seafood	7 kg / **2 kg**
Eggs	12 kg / **2 kg**
Peanuts / tree nuts	4 kg / **0.4 kg**
Sweeteners**	55 kg / **11 kg**
Cheese	13 kg / **2 kg**

*Beef, pork, veal and lamb
**Sugar, corn sweeteners, honey and syrups

*2008, the latest year data is available. Amounts do not include nonedible food parts such as bones, peels, stones and cores.

Four meerkats stand alert in the red sand of the Kalahari Desert, Botswana, ready to warn the rest of the mob at the first sign of a predator.

Money

Before there was money, people bartered trade goods or services for what they considered equal value. Metal in some form may have been used as far back as 2000 B.C. as a convenient, trusted medium of exchange, just as cowrie shells were used in India, wampum (shell beads) in North America and whales' teeth in Fiji. But the first standardised, accepted currency was the coins minted in seventh-century B.C. Lydia, an ancient kingdom in what is now western Turkey. They were bean-shaped pieces of electrum, a natural mixture of gold and silver, stamped to indicate a uniform value regardless of weight. Other countries realised the convenience of a money system and started their own currencies. ■

Herb of the Month

Cayenne

TRADITIONAL USES: Arthritis and nerve pain

History Cayenne peppers, native to Central and South America, were being cultivated in these regions more than 9,000 years ago. Not until the 15th century was cayenne introduced to the rest of the world. Cayenne seeds were first brought to Europe following Columbus's voyage of 1492.

The Maya used it to treat infections, the Aztec to quiet throbbing toothaches. Cayenne has also been used in traditional Ayurvedic, Chinese, Japanese and Korean medicines as a topical for arthritis and muscle pain and as an oral remedy for digestive problems. In modern herbal medicine, cayenne is added to lotions and salves to relieve the pain of osteoarthritis and rheumatoid arthritis, shingles and joint or muscle pain. ■

Strange . . . but True: Space

1. The universe is about 13.7 billion years old.

2. Saucer-shaped lenticular clouds have been mistaken for UFOs.

3. Saturn's rings are made of ice and rocks.

4. The north pole of Uranus gets no sunlight for about 42 years at a time.

5. Our universe has no centre.

6. There is no time at the centre of a black hole.

7. Some of the most expensive rocks on Earth come from the moon.

8. The temperature on the moon can be hotter than boiling water.

9. Saturn would float in water.

10. The surface of the moon is smaller than Asia.

Tinted orange by the morning sun, a soaring dune is the backdrop for these hulks of camel thorn trees in Namib-Naukluft Park, Namibia.

OC

WHEN BERRIES ARE MANY IN OCTOBER, BEWARE A HARD WINTER

TOBER

OCTOBER 2013

1 TUESDAY

2 WEDNESDAY

3 THURSDAY

4 FRIDAY ●

5 SATURDAY

6 SUNDAY

7 MONDAY

8 TUESDAY

9 WEDNESDAY

10 THURSDAY

11 FRIDAY ◐

12 SATURDAY

13 SUNDAY

14 MONDAY

15 TUESDAY

16 WEDNESDAY

17 THURSDAY

18 FRIDAY ○

19 SATURDAY

20 SUNDAY

21 MONDAY

22 TUESDAY

23 WEDNESDAY

24 THURSDAY

25 FRIDAY

26 SATURDAY ◑

27 SUNDAY

28 MONDAY

29 TUESDAY

30 WEDNESDAY

31 THURSDAY

Bird of the Month

Common Quail

(Coturnix coturnix)

LENGTH: 16–18 cm

RANGE: Widespread in the Old World

The word quail finds its origins in the Middle Dutch quacken, meaning 'to croak'. The words quail and quack are related, and the bird's English name is in reference to its distinctive call.

Sudoku Challenge

3								7
4			1	5	2			3
2	8						4	9
			8		7			
9	4			2			3	8
			3		4			
8	3						1	2
5			2	7	8			6
7								4

Answers on p. 156

Both John Glenn, the first American to orbit Earth, and Neil Armstrong carried tiny National Geographic flags with them on their celebrated missions.

A FLAG IN SPACE

National Geographic loaned staff photographer Dean Conger to NASA to make a permanent colour record of the manned space program. Conger's pictures of astronaut Alan Shepard, the first American in space, being plucked from the ocean appeared in newspapers around the world. In 1962 John Glenn became the first American to orbit the Earth and he carried a tiny National Geographic flag with him. National Geographic photographers made historic photos of the launch and recovery.

Neil Armstrong also carried a small National Geographic flag when he became the first person ever to step on the surface of the moon in 1969. In December of that year, the magazine published a five-part package on the feat, featuring photographs of the mission and a small phonographic record, 'Sounds of the Space Age'. ■

The National Geographic Society flag was designed by Elsie May Bell Grosvenor in 1903.

October Constellation

The Great Square of Pegasus, an asterism at the centre of the constellation of the same name, is central to locating Andromeda. Alpheratz is shared by Andromeda and the asterism. Autumn also provides an opportunity to view galaxies, like the Andromeda galaxy (M31), visible to the naked eye.

ANDROMEDA

MAKEUP: 7 stars

BEST VIEWED: Oct/Nov

LOCATION: Autumn, centre of chart

SIZE IN THE SKY: ✋

ALPHA STAR: Alpheratz

DEEP SKY OBJECT: Andromeda galaxy

Mythology In Ancient Greek myth, Princess Andromeda of Ethiopia was chained to a rock as a sacrifice to the gods. Andromeda's mother, Cassiopeia, claimed that her daughter's beauty surpassed that of the daughters of Nereus, god of the sea and father-in-law of Poseidon. Angered by her boasting, Poseidon sent the monster Cetus to destroy the kingdom of Ethiopia until Cassiopeia and her husband Cepheus sacrificed their daughter. The princess was rescued just in time by Perseus.

About To locate the constellation, on autumn evenings trace a line northeast from the northeast corner of the Great Square of Pegasus. The constellation most notably contains the Andromeda galaxy, a spiral-shaped galaxy not unlike our own Milky Way. It is visible to the naked eye, a light splotch just west of her right arm. ■

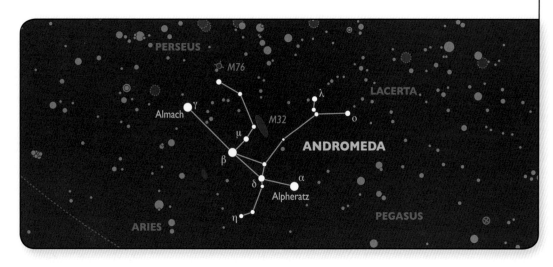

PERSEUS
M76
Almach γ
μ
M32
β
ANDROMEDA
LACERTA
λ
o
δ α
Alpheratz
η
ARIES
PEGASUS

English
LOL = laughing out loud

French
mort de rire = died of laughter

jajaja
Spanish
jajaja = ha ha ha

Dari (spoken in Afghanistan)
ma khanda mikonom = I am laughing

In Malaysia
ha3 = ha times three

Tracking E-Laughs

The most common way to e-laugh is to use an abbreviation that mimics real laughter, says Indiana University linguist Susan Herring. But as the list above shows, e-mirth has many e-guises.

The Flying and Diving Dog

Every dog has his day, but few canines can claim days spent jumping out of aeroplanes and exploring reefs. In a moment most matchmakers can only dream of, Hooch—half King Charles spaniel, half blue heeler, 100 per cent explorer—met the eyes of Sean Herbert—aviation company owner, skydiving instructor and scuba diver—in an Australian pound.

Hooch and her owner, Sean Herbert, enjoy a scuba diving lesson together in Sydney, Australia. Hooch's other hobbies included skydiving.

Hooch began her rise to heights of greatness by racing up the tarmac to a plane just as Herbert was getting on board to take off for a skydive. 'The person by the door grabbed the dog and said, "Is this yours?" as we were taking off,' Herbert remembers. 'The pilot wasn't about to look after a puppy, so I duct-taped her to the inside of my suit, and we jumped. She seemed pretty happy.' Soon enough, Hooch had her own custom-designed harness and was skydiving weekly with her human partner.

When Hooch first saw her master in the water with his scuba gear on, she jumped overboard and began to duck-dive down to him. So Herbert did what any responsible owner would do: he contacted a wetsuit company to custom-make a dog-size outfit for Hooch. But what to do for the mask? Herbert headed to a lighting shop and tried glass lampshades on his dog. 'At first the store owner wasn't happy,' Herbert says. 'But when I explained what I was trying to do he was very helpful.' Engineers came in to attach the casing to oxygen, and soon the pair began training in swimming pools, then moved to small shallows, and finally reefs.

At the ripe old age of 15, Hooch finally succumbed from a genetic fault inherited from her King Charles lineage: as Herbert says of her cardiac arrest, 'Their hearts grow too big for their bodies.' Hooch's body may ultimately have failed her, but her adventurous spirit never flagged whether she was diving from the sky or flying in the sea. ■

STRANGE . . . BUT TRUE!

Scuba divers send postcards from a postbox off the coast of Japan 10 metres underwater.

Geography Q & A

Q **1** Invaded by Turkish forces in 1974, which Mediterranean island is divided between the Turkish-controlled north and the Greek south?

Q **2** What language is spoken by more Chinese than any other language? →

Q **3** The Tropic of Capricorn passes through the largest island in the Indian Ocean. Name this island.

Answers on p. 155

BIOLOGY

Bumblebee Maths

The flight of the bumblebee—even when not set to music—may seem frenetic and random as the workers forage for pollen and nectar to carry home. But researchers at Queen Mary, University of London, discovered there's choreography in the flowerbed. Each bee has a brain the size of a grass seed, but the insects are able to harvest efficiently by solving one of maths' great puzzles: the travelling salesman problem. The challenge is to find the shortest way to visit each flower once before returning to the nest. Computers must resort to laborious calculations, measuring each possible route. The bees studied, *Bombus terrestris,* use spatial memory, rapidly refining routes through trial and error. (Hint: moving to the next nearest flower isn't the answer.) Scientists know *why* the bees do it—flying is exhausting. Now they're trying to figure out *how* they do it. Learning what dictates their decisions could yield insights that improve our transportation and communication networks. ■

In lab trials, bees found the shortest route connecting six flowers without trying all the possible paths. Each bee was tested 80 times and used the shortest route more frequently over time.

32,000-Year-Old Plant Brought Back to Life

The oldest plant ever to be regenerated has been grown from 32,000-year-old seeds, beating the previous record holder by some 30,000 years.

Recently, a Russian team discovered a seed cache of *Silene stenophylla*, a flowering plant native to Siberia that had been buried by an Ice Age squirrel near the banks of the Kolyma River. Radiocarbon dating confirmed that the seeds were 32,000 years old.

The mature and immature seeds, which had been entirely encased in ice, were unearthed from 38 metres (124 feet) below the permafrost, surrounded by layers that included mammoth, bison and woolly rhinoceros bones. The mature seeds had been damaged—perhaps by the squirrel itself prevent them from germinating in the burrow. But so the immature seeds retained viable plant material

The team extracted that tissue from the frozen see vials and successfully germinated the plants, according The plants—identical to each other but with different flower modern *S. stenophylla*—grew, flowered and, after a year, creat their own. 'I can't see any intrinsic fault in the article,' said botanist Raven, President Emeritus of the Missouri Botanical Garden, who wa not involved in the study. 'Though it's such an extraordinary report tha course you'd want to repeat it.' The new study suggests that perma could be a 'depository for an ancient gene pool', a place where a of now extinct species could be found and resurrected, experts sa

Looking good for 32,000 years old. Pictured here, the *Silene stenophylla* has been regenerated from ancient seeds found below the permafrost in Siberia.

Secrets of Shrunken Heads

In 1923 this trophy head arrived at what is now the McManus Museum in Dundee, Scotland. Was it a man or a monkey? Was it authentic? And most intriguingly, what did the original face look like?

The artefact was thought to come from deep in the western Amazon, home to the Shuar people. Also called Jivaro in early descriptions, they believed a slain enemy harboured an avenging spirit that could be overcome only by shrinking the dead person's head and holding related ceremonies. The Shuar believed shrinking the heads of enemies would render them powerless, and they would gain authority over the enemies' wives and children. They are the only known portion of the Amazon jungle-dwelling population to practice the ritual of head shrinking.

As more Europeans entered the region in the late 1800s, such heads, or *tsantsas*, became popular souvenirs. Their fascination with the shrunken heads may have increased local warfare, as warriors sought heads for trade. Fakes soon appeared, some made from animals.

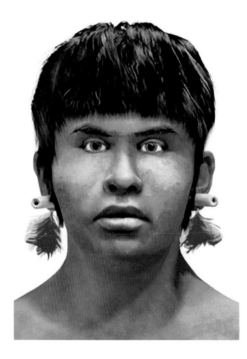

An image created using the latest forensic technology on a shrunken head belonging to the McManus Museum in Dundee allows us to see how the young Shuar warrior may have looked.

To solve the mysteries, University of Dundee forensic art student Tobias Houlton launched a modern investigation. Examining the hair and scalp revealed that the head was human. Details such as the distended lips and the dark, polished skin convinced him that this was a true Shuar creation. He then experimented on pigs, whose skin consistency resembles that of humans, to test the physical effects of head shrinking.

Following the steps documented by a collector who had lived with the Shuar, he found that cartilage resists shrinkage, resulting in the snub-nosed profile typical of tsantsas.

With the assumption that the head belonged to a young warrior, Houlton reconstructed his features using the latest forensic computer tools, as if working as a detective on a police case. No other tsantsa has been brought back to life like this, so the man—whoever he was—has now become the face of a lost tradition. ∎

ACTUAL SIZE

The trophy head features its owner's original hair. The feathers are toucan feathers and are typical of Shuar heads. The Shuar believed that shrinking the head of a slain enemy would overcome its vengeful spirit.

How to Shrink a Head

During a raid a victor would decapitate his fallen enemy. He then made one cut and peeled the skin from the skull, producing a pliable mask of face and hair.

1 HEAT TREATMENT
After the skin soaked in hot water, residual fat was scraped off. The cut was sewn to restore the head's shape and hot stones were dropped into the neck hole.

2 FACE WORK
Hot sand followed the stones, shrinking the head as it dried. The face was smeared with charcoal and ironed smooth with more hot stones.

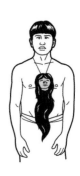

3 WAR TROPHY
Now the size of a large fist, the head was smoked for preservation. A cord attached at the crown allowed it to be worn as a necklace.

A Chondro python, also known as *Morelia viridis* or green tree python, lies curled and watchful. The tree-dwelling snake can be found in New Guinea, Indonesia and parts of northern Australia.

Tea

The apocryphal story about how the Chinese discovered tea involves Emperor Shennong's hygienic belief in boiled water and a few leaves of a plant falling into his cup around the year 2737 B.C. Buddhist monks brought tea from China to Japan a century or so later, where the tea ceremony was developed into a simple but highly formalised ritual that still has a place in Japanese culture today. It took eight centuries more before tea caught on in the West, introduced by Dutch traders. For a while, tea was all the rage at the French court, with one noblewoman writing that a courtier was known to drink 40 cups each morning. However, tea reached England not through French fashion but through King Charles II's marriage to Catherine de Braganza, whose Lisbon upbringing included a passion for tea drinking. ■

NATURAL HEALING

Herb of the Month

Tea

TRADITIONAL USES: Heart health, cholesterol, anti-inflammatory and antioxidant, weight loss, cancer prevention

History Tea's species name, *sinensis*, is a reference to China, where both this bushy shrub and tea culture got their start. The three main varieties of tea—green, oolong and black—owe their differences to variations in processing the leaves. It is primarily green tea that has been used in traditional Chinese and Indian herbal medicine for many centuries. Green tea has long been valued as a stimulant, a diuretic, an astringent to control bleeding and help heal wounds, and a tonic for improving the condition of the heart and blood vessels. Traditionally, green tea was given to promote digestive health and to regulate blood sugar. ■

PUB TRIVIA

Strange ... but True: Cats and Dogs

❶ Cats communicate using at least 16 known 'cat words'.

❷ Cheetahs can change direction in midair when chasing prey.

❸ Catnip can affect lions and tigers.

❹ The chihuahua is the world's smallest dog breed.

❺ Snow leopards can't roar.

❻ A newborn puppy can take up to two months to start wagging its tail.

❼ Cats can't taste sweets.

❽ Lions spend about 20 hours a day resting.

❾ A tiger can eat more than 36 kilograms of meat in one sitting.

❿ A dog can make about 100 different facial expressions.

Putting things into perspective. This man appears to be standing on a spoon in the world's largest salt pan, in Salar de Uyuni, Bolivia.

NOVE

DELICIOUS AUTUMN! MY VERY SOUL IS WEDDED TO IT

MBER

1 FRIDAY

2 SATURDAY

3 SUNDAY ●

4 MONDAY

5 TUESDAY

6 WEDNESDAY

7 THURSDAY

8 FRIDAY

9 SATURDAY

10 SUNDAY ◐

11 MONDAY

12 TUESDAY

13 WEDNESDAY

14 THURSDAY

15 FRIDAY

16 SATURDAY

17 SUNDAY ○

18 MONDAY

19 TUESDAY

20 WEDNESDAY

21 THURSDAY

22 FRIDAY

23 SATURDAY

24 SUNDAY

25 MONDAY ◐

26 TUESDAY

27 WEDNESDAY

28 THURSDAY

29 FRIDAY

30 St Andrew's Day (Scotland)
SATURDAY

Bird of the Month

Bohemian Waxwing

(Bombycilla garrulus)

LENGTH: 18–21 cm

RANGE: Widespread in the northern hemisphere

Waxwing is in reference to the curious red secretions on the bird's wing tip, which resemble the colour of sealing wax. Bombycillidae is a combination of the Greek bombyx, bombykos meaning 'silkworm' and the Latin cilla for 'tail'.

Sudoku Challenge

	8							6
		5	9		4	2		
2			6		1			5
	6	1				9	2	
	3	4				8	5	
8			4		3			1
		6	1		9	4		
	4						9	

Answers on p. 156

National Geographic Society has a long history of sponsoring archaeological expeditions. Here, a reconstructed pot from the 1300s is passed out of Mesa Verde, an ancient site in Colorado, U.S.A.

WHAT LIES BENEATH

The first archaeological expedition sponsored by the National Geographic Society caused great excitement. In 1913 Hiram Bingham reported on the existence of Machu Picchu, an Inca citadel high in the Peruvian Andes. In the 1920s Neil Judd explored the mysterious Pueblo Bonito, 'beautiful village', in New Mexico's Chaco Canyon National Monument. And in the forests of Mexico in the 1930s Matthew Stirling found traces of the Olmec, a pre-Columbian civilization whose colossal stone heads and other mysterious objects are not yet fully understood. More recently, Society-supported archaeologists have gone on to find royal Moche tombs in Peru, the frozen mummy of the 'Inca Ice Maiden' and a staircase covered with hieroglyphs in Honduras. ■

A Thracian battle helmet, dating from the sixth century B.C., excavated in Bulgaria

November Constellation

The Great Square of Pegasus, an asterism at the centre of the constellation of the same name, is central to locating several other autumn constellations. Look for four major meteor showers in the fall: the Orionids in October, the Taurids and Leonids in November and the Geminids in December.

CETUS

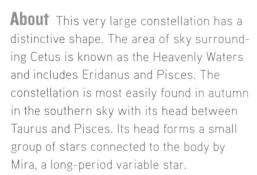

MAKEUP: 13 stars
BEST VIEWED: Nov
LOCATION: Autumn, southeast quadrant
SIZE IN THE SKY: ✋
ALPHA STAR: Menkar
DEEP SKY OBJECT: Mira, variable star

Mythology Sea god Poseidon sent the Cetus to terrorise Ethiopia after being insulted by Queen Cassiopeia's boasting that her daughter was more beautiful than the god's wife.

About This very large constellation has a distinctive shape. The area of sky surrounding Cetus is known as the Heavenly Waters and includes Eridanus and Pisces. The constellation is most easily found in autumn in the southern sky with its head between Taurus and Pisces. Its head forms a small group of stars connected to the body by Mira, a long-period variable star.

Watching Mira can be a worthwhile project and a helpful way to develop a sense of stellar magnitude. At its brightest, the star reaches around magnitude 2.4, but then over 11 months it fades to a magnitude of 9.3—invisible to the naked eye. ■

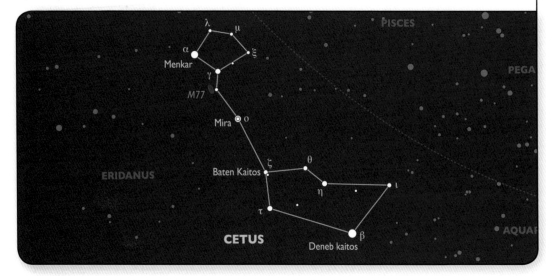

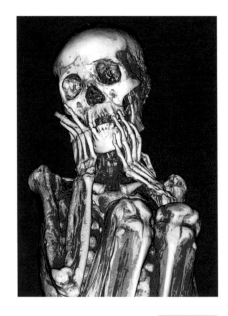

3-D Mummy

A woman was scanned with the newest high-resolution CT technology. She came from the highlands of central Peru—where she died 550 years ago. She's the first complete mummy whose health has been probed by radiologists using such detailed CT images. Radiologists identified signs of tuberculosis or a fungal lung infection.

'White', Albino-like Penguin

Birds of a feather usually flock together—but not in the case of a rare 'white' mutant penguin, spotted in a chinstrap penguin colony in Antarctica. The 'blonde' penguin, seen at the edge of one of the South Shetland Islands, 'astonished' tourists on a National Geographic Journey to Antarctica cruise.

Though the penguin looks like an albino, the bird actually appears to have isabellinism, said penguin expert P. Dee Boersma of the University of Washington in Seattle. The condition is a genetic mutation that dilutes pigment in penguins' feathers, according to a 2009 study on isabellinism published in the journal *Marine Ornithology*. This results in a 'uniform lightening' of a bird's dark colours, turning the animal a greyish yellow or pale brown, the study said.

Although they technically represent separate conditions, the terms 'isabellinism' and 'leucism' are sometimes used interchangeably. Leucism is a mutation that prevents any melanin at all from being produced in feathers. Albinism

Standing out from the crowd, this rare chinstrap penguin discovered in Antarctica has an unusual condition known as isabellinism, according to experts.

STRANGE ... BUT TRUE!

The lowest known temperature on Earth (-89.2 °C) was recorded in Antarctica.

occurs when an animal produces no melanin at all throughout its entire body. 'Many species of penguins have a few rare individuals with this colour pattern,' Boersma said via email. For instance, scientists have observed the most cases of isabellinism in gentoo penguins, which are found throughout the Antarctic Peninsula. Magellanic penguins, which live on South American coasts, seem to have the lowest incidence of the condition.

In the ocean, penguins' black backs camouflage the birds from both predator and prey swimming above, so Boersma suspects isabellinism would affect the South Shetland bird's survival, although there are no studies on the subject, she said. ■

Geography Q&A

← **Q** **1** Which of the following mountain ranges is *not* in Europe—the Pyrenees, Apennines or Pamirs?

Q **2** Which of the following is *not* a trench found in the Pacific Ocean—the Aleutian Trench, the Puerto Rico Trench or the Philippine Trench?

Q **3** Which country is *not* crossed by the Equator—Chad, Colombia or Indonesia?

Answers on p. 155

HEALTH

People Can Hallucinate Colour at Will

In a recent experiment, scientists asked a group of pre-screened people to look at a set of grey patterns and try to visualise colour. Eleven members of the group had been identified as susceptible to hypnosis while seven of the subjects were not susceptible. All the subjects who were easily hypnotised saw a range of colours even while not under hypnosis. MRI scans showed that the parts of the subjects' brains linked to colour perception lit up when they saw the imaginary hues. 'We can see changes in these colour-sensitive regions of their brains, which they have no way of faking,' said William McGeown, a neuroscientist at the U.K.'s Hull University. The study found that being under hypnosis enhanced colour hallucination in susceptible subjects. ■

Brain scans have confirmed that the power of suggestion can let some people see imaginary colours, particularly if they are susceptible to hypnosis.

The Wondrous Coconut

Don't knock it, the coconut comes in a perfect package. For millions of years the tropical fruit has populated islands by floating from shore to shore in a buoyant husk. That packaging, it turns out, also helps it navigate the U.S. postal system. Mailing a coconut in the U.S.A. is surprisingly simple: pen address on surface, affix postage, and off it goes.

Each year some 3,000 'coconut postcards' get shipped this way from Hawaii's Hoolehua post office. But creativity can come from anywhere. Other self-contained mailings have included pumpkins, driftwood, flip-flops and messages in sand-filled bottles. The U.S. Postal Service tries to deliver so long as objects don't pose a risk, says spokeswoman Sue Brennan. 'Can you mail a dog? We get this question all the time,' she says. 'The answer is, no!'

Postcard, health drink, shredded sweet, woven mat, biofuel—is there anything a coconut can't become? Humans have used this versatile palm-tree 'nut' for half a million years, by one estimate. Even so, coconuts remain refreshingly cutting-edge.

Take their appeal as an energy source. This year Tokelau, a trio of South Pacific atolls, aims to generate all of its power with solar energy and coconut oil. It joins other coconut-rich places—including Papua New Guinea, the Philippines and Vanuatu—that have blended or modified coconut oil to run things like ships, trucks and official vehicles. On the health front, electrolyte-packed coconut water has been making waves in the U.S. and Brazil, where packaged consumption doubled from 2005 to 2010. Call it a gourmet turn for a hydrating drink long enjoyed straight from the shell. ∎

The perfect package. A coconut covered in stamps arrives safely at *National Geographic* magazine's head office via the U.S. Postal Service.

Crocodiles' Powerful Chompers

Crocodiles may be the world's champion chompers, killing with the greatest bite force ever directly measured for living animals, a new study says. In fact, their bite force may rival that of mighty *T. rex*.

Paleobiologist Gregory M. Erickson and colleagues put all 23 living crocodilian species through an unprecedented bite test. The 'winners'—saltwater crocodiles—slammed their jaws shut with 3,700 pounds per square inch (psi), or 16,460 newtons, of bite force. By contrast, you might tear into a steak with 150 to 200 psi (890 newtons). Hyenas, lions and tigers generate around 1,000 psi (4,450 newtons).

And while a 2008 computer model estimated that a 6.5-metre great white shark would produce nearly 4,000 psi (17,790 newtons) of bite force, that figure hasn't been directly measured.

Erickson and colleagues did physically measure the bites of several 5-metre saltwater crocs—as well as Nile crocodiles, alligators, caimans, gharials and other crocs, some for the first time ever. The team spent countless

Dr. Gregory M. Erickson demonstrates the very resilient equipment that allowed him and his team to test and compare the incredible bite forces of 23 species of crocodile.

hours wrestling with the reptiles at Florida's St. Augustine Alligator Farm Zoological Park and getting them to bite a force transducer—a 'very expensive, very durable, waterproof bathroom scale that's padded with leather'.

'The testing is like dragon slaying by committee, often involving ten or more people to test a single animal,' said Erickson, of Florida State University. For every croc species, the transducer registered impressive power, suggesting that a big bite is at the heart of what it means to be a crocodilian, according to Erickson. 'That's why I think they've been so successful,' he said. 'They have seized on a remarkable design for producing bite force and pressure to occupy ecological niches on the water's edge for 85 million years, and no one else evolved that could wrest those niches from them.'

Surprisingly, at least to Erickson, variations in the bite forces of croc species turn out to be largely based on body size. In many animal groups this variation is tied to differing jaw shapes and tooth forms, but those features didn't much affect the croc bites in the team's tests. ∎

The bigger the croc, the bigger the bite. The force with which a crocodile can bite down is dependent on its overall body size rather than the size of its jaw, the team found.

EDITOR'S PICK

Revellers celebrate the vibrant Hindu festival of Holi. In this joyous celebration of the coming of spring, people smear each other with bright-coloured powders known as Gulal.

Poker

Although poker originated in Europe, it became established and popularised in the United States and then spread back across the Atlantic. Card games similar to poker were developed by the 1520s. The Spanish three-card game *primero* included betting on high hands—three of a kind, a pair and a *flux* (flush), or three of the same suit.

By the year 1700 there were a number of five-card games that involved not only betting but also bluffing—betting on a bad hand to trick others into folding, or dropping out. The word *poker* derives from *poque*, which itself is a corruption of *pochen* ('to bluff'). Good players develop a 'poker face', or unreadable bluff. ■

Herb of the Month

Grapes, Grape Seed

TRADITIONAL USES: Heart health and antioxidant

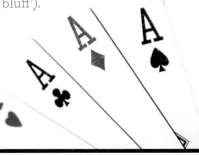

History Scenes of grape harvesting and winemaking decorate many Egyptian tombs, revealing the importance of *Vitis vinifera* in ancient Egypt by at least 2700 B.C. Seven hundred years later, Phoenician sailors were transporting grapevines across the Mediterranean to Greece. From there, grapes and grape growing spread to Europe and the rest of the world.

Both grapes and wine have been lauded as food and medicine for thousands of years. Roman physician Pliny the Elder (A.D. 23–79) praised the gods for 'bestowing healing powers on the vine'. Today, research has shown that many health-promoting properties are contained in grape seeds, rich in antioxidants. ■

Strange . . . but True: Weather

1. There have been at least four major ice ages.

2. There are about 16 million thunderstorms on Earth every year.

3. A snowflake can take up to two hours to fall from a cloud to the ground.

4. From about 21 March to 23 September the sun never sets at the North Pole.

5. Almost 90 per cent of snow is air.

6. In the open ocean, a tsunami sometimes travels as fast as a jet plane.

7. Tornadoes usually spin in opposite directions above and below the Equator.

8. Snowflakes get smaller as the temperature drops.

9. A cloud can weigh more than a million pounds, or 453,593 kilograms.

10. There are about 3,000 lightning flashes on Earth every minute.

An Adélie penguin takes a flying leap from an iceberg near Brown Bluff, Antarctica. Its modified wings propel the bird elegantly through the water, but unfortunately are much less useful in the air.

DECF

WINTER DRAWS OUT WHAT SUMMER LAID IN

MBER

1 SUNDAY

2 St Andrew's Day Bank Holiday (Scotland)
MONDAY

3 TUESDAY ●

4 WEDNESDAY

5 THURSDAY

6 FRIDAY

7 SATURDAY

8 SUNDAY

9 MONDAY ◐

10 TUESDAY

11 WEDNESDAY

12 THURSDAY

13 FRIDAY

14 SATURDAY

15 SUNDAY

16 MONDAY

17 TUESDAY ○

18 WEDNESDAY

19 THURSDAY

20 FRIDAY

21 SATURDAY

22 SUNDAY

23 MONDAY

24 TUESDAY

25 Christmas Day
WEDNESDAY ◐

26 Boxing Day
THURSDAY

27 FRIDAY

28 SATURDAY

29 SUNDAY

30 MONDAY

31 TUESDAY

Bird of the Month

Pintail *(Anas acuta)*

LENGTH: 51–62 cm
RANGE: Widespread in the northern hemisphere

The word anas is derived from the Latin word nature, for 'swim', and means 'duck'. Acuta comes from the Latin for 'pointed' and is a useful field mark referring to the duck's pointed tail.

GEO PUZZLE

Sudoku Challenge

	9						1	
8			1		2			3
3	2						6	8
9				7				1
	8		9		6		3	
1				3				5
5	1						7	4
6			7		5			9
	3					5		

Answers on p. 156

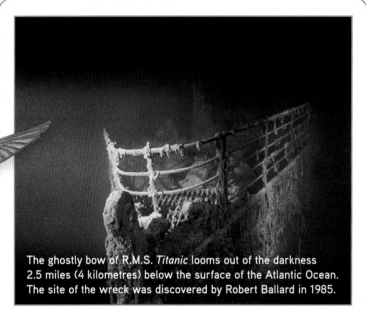

The ghostly bow of R.M.S. *Titanic* looms out of the darkness 2.5 miles (4 kilometres) below the surface of the Atlantic Ocean. The site of the wreck was discovered by Robert Ballard in 1985.

RE-DISCOVERING *TITANIC*

Built in Belfast, the 270-metre-long luxury liner R.M.S. *Titanic* was the world's largest passenger ship when it was launched in 1912. On its maiden voyage, *Titanic* hit an iceberg and sank, killing more than 1,500 people. In 1985, Bob Ballard made an amazing discovery. 'I cannot believe my eyes,' he wrote in the December 1985 edition of *National Geographic*. 'From the abyss two and a half miles beneath the sea the bow of a great vessel emerges in ghostly detail.' It was the remains of *Titanic*, the most exciting shipwreck discovery of the time. Around the world, Bob Ballard became a household name. Ballard believes the shipwreck site should remain undisturbed as a 'sacred grave'. ∎

Stopped for eternity— a pocket watch that was recovered just after *Titanic* sank records the moment of tragedy.

December Constellation

The ancient astronomers who organised the zodiac noted that the sun was 'in' Aries at the vernal equinox—meaning it was travelling in the Ram's part of the sky on the day when it passed from the southern to the northern celestial sphere for the year.

ARIES

MAKEUP: 4 stars

BEST VIEWED: Nov/Dec

LOCATION: Winter, southwest quadrant

SIZE IN THE SKY: ✋

ALPHA STAR: Hamal

DEEP SKY OBJECT: Gamma Arietis, double star

Mythology Aries was widely recognised as a ram—despite being made of only four stars. According to the Greeks, Aries was the source of the golden fleece stolen by Jason and the Argonauts. The ram was sent to rescue two children of a king from an abusive stepmother. When the ram returned, the grateful king sacrificed it and left the fleece in the custody of a dragon, from where it was stolen by Jason.

About Precession has since shifted this constellation's position with respect to the sun's equatorial crossing, but by tradition Aries remains where the zodiac begins. On evenings in late autumn and early winter, Aries is high in the east, between the Great Square of Pegasus and the Pleiades in Taurus. The tail of the Ram is represented by the star Gamma Arietis, a double star with a wide, eight-arc-second separation between the two members. It was one of the first doubles spotted with a telescope—by astronomer Robert Hooke in 1664. ◾

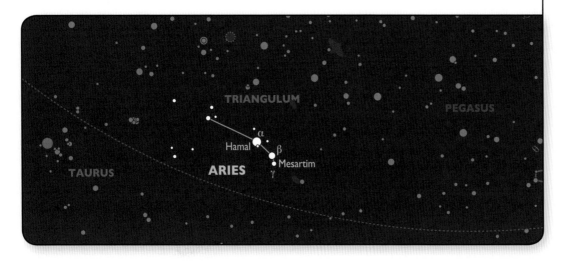

TRIANGULUM

PEGASUS

Hamal

α

β

Mesartim

γ

ARIES

TAURUS

Heroic Mum

During a flash flood along Malaysia's Segama River, a conservation group encountered a stranded orangutan mother and baby. In order to help the pair they tied a rope to a tree and tossed the mum the free end. With her baby clinging to her back, the mother grasped the rope and crossed the rushing waters safely, with baby in tow.

The Evolution of Angels

'Tis the season for winged humanoids to alight everywhere from shop windows to Christmas tree tops to lingerie runways. Angels, at least the Christian variety, haven't always been flying people in diaphanous gowns. And their various forms—from disembodied minds to feathered guardians—reflect twists and turns of thousands of years of religious thought.

There is lots of interesting theology about angels, and in some ways we've kind of lost the knack for that,' said John Cavadini, chair of theology at the University of Notre Dame. 'We tend to think of angels as things that we'd find in a Hallmark card,' Cavadini added. 'But many people, especially in antiquity, were very interested in them'—in what they might look like, how they might organize themselves, how they behave.

In the Bible angels served as envoys of God—*angelos* being Greek for 'messenger'. Other than that, the Scriptures leave a lot of room for interpretation. 'There isn't a lot

of detail, and that's the fascinating thing,' said Ellen Muehlberger, a professor of Middle Eastern studies at the University of Michigan.

In the early days of Christianity, some believers considered Jesus Christ himself to be one of many angels, said Muehlberger. 'We only know about this because of later, fourth-century authors who penned negative descriptions of this belief' to refute it, she said. Jesus officially lost his angelhood when the Roman emperor Constantine I convened the Council of Nicea in 325. The Council of Nicea defined Christ as totally divine, as of the same substance as God,' Muehlberger said. 'Christians who worked to interpret the council's decrees over the next several decades took this to mean that Christ was not an angel. Angels were something else entirely.'

Around the same time, debate swirled over just whom angels served on Earth.

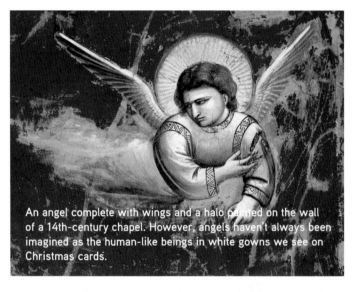

An angel complete with wings and a halo painted on the wall of a 14th-century chapel. However, angels haven't always been imagined as the human-like beings in white gowns we see on Christmas cards.

At early Christian monasteries, for instance, many ascetics assumed that really good pupils would get some kind of divine guide or coach to help them. 'These monks said, hey, not everybody gets a guardian angel—it's a mark of moral success,' said Muehlberger, citing monastic letters from the period explaining the need for monastery inhabitants to cultivate their own angels. Of course, not all angels are angelic, according to some Christian traditions. Satan himself, it's been said, was once an angel named Lucifer. ■

STRANGE ... BUT TRUE!

Palm trees grew at the North Pole about 55 million years ago.

Geography Q & A

Q **1** Which Canadian province produces more than half of the country's manufactured goods?

← **Q** **2** Over the past 100 years, more than 80 per cent of the ice has melted from the summit of Mount Kilimanjaro in which country?

Q **3** Sunflower oil is produced from crops that grow north of Sofia, a city located in which European country?

Answers on p. 155

Answers on p. 155

LANGUAGE

Brave New Words

How does a word get into the venerable *Oxford English Dictionary*? Wide, long use is key. New-words editor Fiona McPherson enlists a small army of readers to comb through books, magazines, newspapers and various online sources. Fresh words or meanings (such as those on the right) are added to a database and their usages tracked for up to ten years.

If 'cankle', for instance, pops up often enough, it may be one of the 4,000 words—out of 6,000 considered—that make the cut each year. Then it will be there to stay. 'The *OED* is unique,' says McPherson, 'in that we never remove a word once it has been included.' ∎

pep · pi · er
\pe-pē-'yā\
n : a waiter whose sole job is to offer diners ground pepper, usually from a large pepper mill

face palm
\'fās ,päm\
n : an expression of exasperation or disbelief

← **drin · gle** \'driŋ-gəl\
n : the watermark or stain left on wood or paper by a glass of liquid

Every year 4,000 new words, such as 'dringle', are selected for inclusion in the *Oxford English Dictionary* out of a list of 6,000.

It's Official: Stonehenge Stones Were Imported

Some of the volcanic bluestones in the inner ring of Stonehenge officially match an outcrop in Wales that's 160 miles (257 kilometres) from the world-famous site, geologists have reported.

The discovery leaves two big ideas standing about how the massive pieces of the monument arrived at Salisbury Plain: entirely by human hand, or partly by glacier.

As it looks today, 5,000-year-old Stonehenge has an outer ring of 20- to 30-ton sandstone blocks and an inner ring and horseshoe of 3- to 5-ton volcanic bluestone blocks. The monument's larger outer blocks, called the Sarsen stones, were likely quarried some 20 to 30 miles away, where sandstone is a common material.

The origin of the bluestones, however, has weighed heavy on the hearts of archaeologists. Rocks resembling the material under a microscope haven't been found anywhere relatively near Stonehenge—at least until now. 'There's no way of explaining how these stones were transported without knowing where they came from,' said study co-author Robert Ixer of the University of Leicester in the U.K. The new find leaves two prominent theories for how the Welsh rocks got to Salisbury. Humans could have quarried the site and dragged the blocks on wooden rafts. Or a giant glacier may have chiselled off the blocks and ferried them about a hundred miles (160 kilometres) towards Stonehenge, with humans dragging them the rest of the way. ∎

A beautiful image of the ancient site of Stonehenge, Wiltshire, at sunset. Exactly how the huge stones were transported there may remain a mystery.

Piranhas' Bark Worse Than Their Bite?

Piranhas, it turns out, can be excellent communicators, a new study suggests. But don't get the idea they're going soft—their barks, croaks and clicks likely mean 'Leave me alone', 'I might bite you', or 'Now I'm really angry!'

Researchers knew picking up red-bellied piranhas—among the few piranhas dangerous to humans—could prompt croaks from the fish. Even so, no one had studied their sounds in water or provided good evidence for the barks' evolutionary role. Now a fish tank, an underwater microphone and a video camera have helped uncover three different piranha calls, all tied to a variety of grumpy behaviours. 'We knew piranhas were able to make sounds but were not satisfied with the explanation for how they do it,' said biologist Eric Parmentier of the Université de Liège in Belgium. 'We wanted to know how they do this and what these sounds might mean to other fish.'

Twenty-five species of piranha exist in the wild today, but only 'two or three' species pose a threat to humans, Parmentier said. In particular, the red-bellied piranha's voracious appetite

A recent study has shown that the range of noises made by the red-bellied piranha—known for its voracious appetite for fresh meat—help it to communicate with and warn other fish.

for fresh meat is a big reason many scientists have shied away from studying any in-water vocalisations, he added.

Parmentier and study co-author Sandie Millot of the University of Algarve in Portugal used their tech-heavy technique to link three distinct sounds to three aggressive piranha behaviours. A repetitive grunt was tied to a visual faceoff, as if to say, 'Get away from me.' A second call resembling a low thud was associated with circling and fighting with other fish. Both of these calls were made using a fast-twitching muscle that runs along a piranha's swim bladder—an air-filled organ that helps fish maintain their buoyancy.

If fellow piranhas didn't heed these warning calls, the aggressor would begin chasing the neighbouring fish and making a third type of sound by faintly gnashing teeth. In the future, Parmentier and Millot would like to go to South America to record the red-bellied piranhas in their native environment. 'The nature of these fish is quite special, and I suspect they can make more than three sounds,' Parmentier said, adding that they may also use them for hunting or mating. 'Also, there are only recordings for a few species of piranhas. We'd like to see what other species are capable of.' ■

In piranha language, a repetitive grunt means 'get away from me', a low thud is made when circling and fighting with other fish, and gnashing teeth is for when the piranha really means business.

EDITOR'S PICK

Positively radiant, a Cuban tree
frog clings calmly to its perch,
despite having gulped a Christmas light. The frog survived
its brief illumination, and the
image's photographer gently
removed the light.

Christmas stockings

Legend has it that an impoverished nobleman with three daughters could not afford dowries for them. When St. Nicholas heard about their plight, he dropped three bags of gold coins down the family's chimney, which landed in the girls' stockings hung by the hearth to dry. Since then, children have hung their stockings from fireplace mantels or other places in the house in order to receive presents from St. Nick/Santa Claus. ■

Herb of the Month

Peppermint

TRADITIONAL USES: Indigestion, irritable bowel syndrome, colds and coughs, muscle aches, tension headache

History Peppermint is the aromatic plant that gives the sweets of the same name their cool, refreshing taste. It is one of more than two dozen species of mint that belong to the genus *Mentha*. The name comes from Minthe, a nymph in Greek mythology who had the misfortune to be loved by Hades, god of the underworld, and subsequently was turned into an insignificant little plant by Hades' jealous wife. According to the story, Hades tried to make it up to Minthe by sweetly scenting her small green leaves.

While several mints appear to have been cultivated since the time of the ancient Egyptians, peppermint is a relative newcomer. It was discovered in England in 1696, a natural hybrid of two other mint species. Cultivation of peppermint spread rapidly across Europe, and colonists transported the herb to the New World. Today, peppermint ranks near the top of the world's favourite flavourings. It is also a respected herbal remedy for an upset stomach and other digestive issues. ■

Strange but True Birds

1. Parrots talk without vocal cords.
2. Most swans in England belong to the Queen.
3. Some geese can soar to 9,750 m—high enough to see a 747 passenger jet fly by.
4. A rooster is also called a chanticleer.
5. Birds don't sweat.
6. Some parrots dance when they hear music.
7. A flamingo can eat only when its head is upside down.
8. Some birds can use their bill measure the temperature of th
9. Some baby birds use claws on th wings to climb trees.
10. Penguins swim up to 3,000 miles in a year.

Geography Q&A Answers

JANUARY
Page 16

1 The Gulf of Riga is part of which European sea? *Baltic Sea*

2 Name the mountain range that stretches from the Bay of Biscay to the Mediterranean Sea. *Pyrennes*

3 What country that borders Guatemala has English as its official language? *Belize*

FEBRUARY
Page 28

1 What term is used for the often triangular-shaped deposit of sediment sometimes found at the mouth of a river? *Delta*

2 What is the term for the point on Earth's surface directly above the place where an earthquake originates? *Epicentre*

3 A moraine is made up of soil, rocks and other materials that have been deposited by the action of what kind of physical feature? *Glacier/ice sheet*

MARCH
Page 40

1 The Vistula River and Bialowieza National Park—northern Europe's largest virgin forest and home to the European bison—are in which country? *Poland*

2 What city is home to the building pictured on the right, designed by famed architect Antoni Gaudí? *Barcelona*

3 To visit the ruins of Persepolis, an ancient ceremonial capital of Persia, you would have to travel to what present-day country? *Iran*

APRIL
Page 52

1 The samba, which was originally brought from Africa, is a dance that was adapted and is highly popular on which other continent? *South America*

2 In ancient times the papyrus plant, used for making paper, grew along the Nile River Delta in which country? *Egypt*

3 Afrikaners are the descendants of European settlers who mostly live in which present-day African country? *South Africa*

MAY
Page 64

1 People in the most populous Scandinavian country celebrate a festival of lights called St. Lucia Day to mark the start of the Christmas season. Name this country. *Sweden*

2 Sanskrit, preserved in Hindu sacred writings, is an ancient language in which country? *India*

3 The Gold Museum, which contains a large collection of pre-Columbian gold objects, is in the capital city east of the Magdalena River. Name this city. *Bogota*

JUNE
Page 76

1 The leading grain crop in Bangladesh is a staple food for the country's people. Name this grain. *Rice*

2 Spain's chief industrial city is a Mediterranean port near the country's border with France. Name this city. *Barcelona*

3 Most of Denmark's oil reserves are found in which sea? *North Sea*

JULY

Page 88

1 Which British county is the home of Cheddar cheese? *Somerset*

2 Which country moved its capital from Istanbul to the more centrally located Ankara in the early 20th century? *Turkey*

3 To visit the home of the famous painter Rubens and to walk through the world's largest diamond district in Antwerp, you would travel to which country? *Belgium*

AUGUST

Page 100

1 What theory explains the shifting positions and ongoing movements of the continents? *plate tectonics/continental drift*

2 What is the term for an area of desert where an underground water source supports vegetation growth? *oasis*

3 What Norwegian word is used for a narrow, steep-sided inlet of the sea that was carved by a glacier? *fjord*

SEPTEMBER

Page 112

1 Scientists believe that about 120 million years ago, South America began to break away from which other continent? *Africa*

2 The world's longest coral reef is in the Pacific Ocean off the northeast coast of which continent? *Australia*

3 Which continent produces the largest total amount of rice? *Asia*

OCTOBER

Page 124

1 Invaded by Turkish forces in 1974, which Mediterranean island is divided between the Turkish-controlled north and the Greek south? *Cyprus*

2 What language is spoken by more Chinese than any other language? *Mandarin*

3 The Tropic of Capricorn passes through the largest island in the Indian Ocean. Name this island. *Madagascar*

NOVEMBER

Page 136

1 Which of the following mountain ranges is *not* in Europe—the Pyrenees, Apennines or Pamirs? *Pamirs*

2 Which of the following is *not* a trench found in the Pacific Ocean—the Aleutian Trench, the Puerto Rico Trench or the Philippine Trench? *Puerto Rico Trench*

3 Which country is *not* crossed by the Equator—Chad, Colombia or Indonesia? *Chad*

DECEMBER

Page 148

1 Which Canadian province produces more than half of the country's manufactured goods? *Ontario*

2 Over the past 100 years, more than 80 per cent of the ice has melted from the summit of Mount Kilimanjaro in which country? *Tanzania*

3 Sunflower oil is produced from crops that grow north of Sofia, a city located in which European country? *Bulgaria*

Sudoku Challenge Answers

JANUARY — Page 13

```
1 6 9 5 2 7 8 3 4
8 4 5 9 1 3 7 6 2
3 2 7 6 8 4 1 9 5
2 1 6 8 7 9 5 4 3
9 7 8 3 4 5 6 2 1
4 5 3 1 6 2 9 8 7
7 9 1 2 3 8 4 5 6
5 3 4 7 9 6 2 1 8
6 8 2 4 5 1 3 7 9
```

MAY — Page 61

```
3 8 7 4 6 2 9 5 1
5 6 9 3 8 1 4 7 2
2 4 1 7 5 9 3 8 6
1 2 4 8 3 5 0 0 7
7 3 6 9 1 4 0 2 0
8 9 5 6 2 7 0 0 4
0 0 2 5 9 8 7 4 3
0 5 0 1 7 3 2 6 9
9 0 0 2 4 6 8 1 5
```

SEPTEMBER — Page 109

```
2 3 6 1 4 5 7 8 9
1 9 5 8 6 7 2 3 4
4 7 8 2 9 3 5 6 1
6 8 1 7 5 9 3 4 2
7 2 4 6 3 8 1 9 5
3 5 9 4 1 2 6 7 8
9 1 7 3 2 4 8 5 6
8 4 2 5 7 6 9 1 3
5 6 3 9 8 1 4 2 7
```

FEBRUARY — Page 25

```
7 4 6 3 9 1 8 2 5
2 1 8 4 7 5 9 6 3
5 3 9 2 6 8 7 1 4
3 7 1 8 5 9 6 4 2
8 6 4 7 3 2 5 9 1
9 2 5 6 1 4 3 7 8
1 8 7 5 2 6 4 3 9
4 9 3 1 8 7 2 5 6
6 5 2 9 4 3 1 8 7
```

JUNE — Page 73

```
9 3 4 2 5 1 6 7 8
7 8 6 3 4 9 5 1 2
2 5 1 8 6 7 9 3 4
6 1 9 7 2 4 8 5 3
8 2 5 6 9 3 1 4 7
4 7 3 5 1 8 2 9 6
1 6 7 9 3 2 4 8 5
5 9 8 4 7 6 3 2 1
3 4 2 1 8 5 7 6 9
```

OCTOBER — Page 121

```
1 3 6 4 8 9 5 7 2
9 4 7 1 5 2 6 3 8
5 2 8 7 3 6 4 9 1
3 6 5 8 9 7 2 1 4
7 9 4 5 2 1 3 8 6
8 1 2 3 6 4 7 5 9
6 8 3 9 4 5 1 2 7
4 5 1 2 7 8 9 6 3
2 7 9 6 1 3 8 4 5
```

MARCH — Page 37

```
5 6 4 9 1 8 7 3 2
7 3 2 4 5 6 1 9 8
9 8 1 2 7 3 5 6 4
3 1 9 6 8 2 4 7 5
6 5 7 3 4 1 2 8 9
4 2 8 5 9 7 3 1 6
1 4 5 0 0 0 8 2 3
2 7 6 0 3 0 9 5 1
8 9 3 1 0 5 6 4 7
```

JULY — Page 85

```
3 2 9 8 6 4 1 5 7
4 5 1 9 2 7 3 8 6
7 8 6 1 5 3 2 9 4
2 6 5 7 1 9 4 3 8
8 7 3 2 4 5 9 6 1
9 1 4 3 8 6 5 7 2
6 9 2 5 7 1 8 4 3
1 3 7 4 9 8 6 2 5
5 4 8 6 3 2 7 1 9
```

NOVEMBER — Page 133

```
4 8 7 2 3 5 1 6 9
6 1 5 9 7 4 2 3 8
2 9 3 6 8 1 7 4 5
5 6 1 3 4 8 9 2 7
7 2 8 5 9 6 3 1 4
9 3 4 7 1 2 8 5 6
8 5 9 4 2 3 6 7 1
3 7 6 1 5 9 4 8 2
1 4 2 8 6 7 5 9 3
```

APRIL — Page 49

```
5 9 8 1 2 3 4 7 6
6 4 1 8 9 7 5 2 3
3 7 2 5 6 4 1 9 8
8 3 6 2 4 9 7 5 1
2 1 4 7 5 8 3 6 9
7 5 9 6 3 1 2 8 4
4 8 5 3 7 6 9 1 2
9 6 7 4 1 2 8 3 5
1 2 3 9 8 5 6 4 7
```

AUGUST — Page 97

```
6 3 2 1 4 8 7 5 9
7 5 8 9 3 2 4 1 6
1 9 4 5 6 7 8 3 2
9 4 7 3 8 5 2 6 1
2 1 5 7 9 6 3 8 4
3 8 6 2 1 4 5 9 7
5 2 1 6 7 3 9 4 8
4 6 3 8 2 9 1 7 5
8 7 9 4 5 1 6 2 3
```

DECEMBER — Page 145

```
4 6 9 3 8 7 1 5 2
8 5 7 1 6 2 9 4 3
3 2 1 4 5 9 7 6 8
9 3 6 5 7 4 2 8 1
2 8 5 9 1 6 4 3 7
1 7 4 2 3 8 6 9 5
5 1 2 6 9 3 8 7 4
6 4 8 7 2 5 3 1 9
7 9 3 8 4 1 5 2 6
```

Illustrations Credits

Front cover, Justin Black/Shutterstock; Front cover (INSET), James L. Stanfield; back cover, Ralph Lee Hopkins/National Geographic Stock; 4-5, Frans Lanting/National Geographic Stock; 6, Jimmy Chin and Lynsey Dyer/National Geographic Stock; 8, Jimmy Hoffman/National Geographic My Shot; 10-1, Kristín Jónsdóttir; 13 (LE), David Quinn; 13 (LORT), National Geographic Stock; 13 (UPRT), Stanley Meltzoff/National Geographic Stock; 14 (CTR), Brown Reference Group; 14 (LO), Wil Tirion; 14 (UPLE), thrashem/Shutterstock; 14 (UPRT), Nieves Oaoa Tekki, Fligus Design/National Geographic Stock; 15 (LE), M. Khebra/Shutterstock; 15 (RT), Steven Kazlowski/Alaska Stock Images/National Geographic Stock; 16 (LO), Van J. Wedeen, Harvard, Martinos Center; 16 (UPLE), 3d brained/Shutterstock; 16 (UPRT), asterix0597/iStockphoto; 17 (all), Rebecca Hale, NGP; 18, Marilyn Barbone/Shutterstock; 19, NinaMalyna/Shutterstock; 20, Chris Gibbs/National Geographic My Shot; 21 (LOLE), LianeM/Shutterstock; 21 (RT), tratong/Shutterstock; 21 (UPLE), Nadezda/Shutterstock; 22-3, Alan Sailer/Whitehotpix/Zuma Press; 25 (LE), David Quinn; 25 (LORT), National Geographic Stock; 25 (UPRT), Shekar Dattatri, Conservation India; 26 (CTR), Brown Reference Group; 26 (LO), Wil Tirion; 26 (UPLE), thrashem/Shutterstock; 26 (UPRT), Science/American Association for the Advancement of Science; 27 (LE), Michal Ninger/Shutterstock; 27 (LORT), luckypic/Shutterstock; 27 (UPRT) Denis Barbulat/Shutterstock; 28 (CTR), Julian de Dios/Shutterstock; 28 (LO), Eric Isselée/Shutterstock; 28 (UP), 3d brained/Shutterstock; 29, Doug Perrine/Alamy; 30, Sebastian Kaulitzki/Shutterstock; 31, Rebecca Hale, NGP; 32, George Quiroga/National Geographic My Shot; 33 (LOLE), Heike Rau/Shutterstock; 33 (RT), Dan Exton/Shutterstock; 33 (UPLE), Michael Ledray/Shutterstock; 34-5, Joel Sartore/National Geographic Stock; 37 (LE), David Quinn; 37 (LORT), Photo by Mark Thiessen/National Geographic; 37 (UPRT), Photo by Mark Thiessen/National Geographic; 38 (CTR), Brown Reference Group; 38 (LO), Wil Tirion; 38 (UPLE), thrashem/Shutterstock; 38 (UPRT), Bettmann/Corbis; 39 (CTR), Frank Glaw; 39 (LO), Camilla Wisbauer/iStockphoto.com; 40 (CTR), sportgraphic/Shutterstock.com; 40 (RT), Smit/Shutterstock; 40 (UP), 3d brained/Shutterstock; 41, Hernan Canellas/National Geographic Stock; 42, SipaPhoto/Shutterstock; 42-3, Roadrunners Internationale; 43 (LO), Central Intelligence Agency; 43 (UP), Central Intelligence Agency; 44, Chris Gray/National Geographic My Shot; 45 (LOLE), Only Fabrizio/Shutterstock; 45 (RT), MarcelClemens/Shutterstock; 45 (UPLE), Subbotina Anna/Shutterstock; 46-7, Juhani Kosonen; 49 (LE), David Quinn; 49 (LORT), Robert E. Peary Collection, NGS; 49 (UPRT), jele/Shutterstock; 50 (CTR), Brown Reference Group; 50 (LO), Wil Tirion; 50 (UPLE), thrashem/Shutterstock; 50 (UPRT), Mitsuaki Iwago/Minden Pictures/National Geographic Stock; 51 (LE), photobank.ch/Shutterstock; 51 (RT), Science Pictures Ltd./Photo Researchers, Inc.; 52 (LOLE), Oliver Munday/National Geographic Society; 52 (RT), Pecold/Shutterstock; 52 (UPLE), 3d brained/Shutterstock; 53, Chris Huss/www.chrishuss.com; 53 (INSET), Cheryl Graham/iStockphoto; 54, Andrew Richards, Bohart Museum of Entomology; 55, Andrew Richards, Bohart Museum of Entomology; 56, Pramod Bansode/National Geographic My Shot; 57 (LOLE), Alena Brozova/iStockphoto; 57 (RT), originalpunkt/Shutterstock; 57 (UPLE), Thomas Mounsey/Shutterstock; 58-9, Jasper Juinen/Getty Images; 61 (LE), David Quinn; 61 (LORT), Jim Fagiolo/Mallory & Irvine/Getty Images; 61 (UPRT), NGS Archives; 62 (CTR), Brown Reference Group; 62 (LO), Wil Tirion; 62 (UPLE), thrashem/Shutterstock; 62 (UPRT), German/iStockphoto; 63 (LO), Danomyte/Shutterstock; 63 (UP), Johan Swanepoel/Shutterstock; 64 (CTR), javarman/Shutterstock; 64 (LO), Cameron McIntire; 64 (UP), 3d brained/Shutterstock; 65, Elisabeth Daynes/National Geographic Stock; 66, Joel Sartore; 67, Martin Withers/FLPA/Minden Pictures; 68, Scott Weller/National Geographic My Shot; 69 (LOLE), Vitaly Korovin/Shutterstock; 69 (RT), Robert Red/Shutterstock; 69 (UPLE), Morgan Lane Photography/Shutterstock; 70-1, Miguel Villagran/Getty Images; 73 (LE), David Quinn; 73 (LORT), W. H. Longley and Charles Martin/National Geographic Stock; 73 (UPRT), Brian J. Skerry/National Geographic Stock; 74 (LE CTR), Brown Reference Group; 74 (RT CTR), Wil Tirion; 74 (UPLE), thrashem/Shutterstock; 74 (UPRT), Taro Yamasaki/Time & Life Pictures/Getty Images; 75 (LE), Biosphoto/Alain Compost; 75 (RT), Emin Ozkan/Shutterstock; 76 (LOLE), UniqueLight/Shutterstock; 76 (RT), zirconicusso/Shutterstock; 76 (UPLE), 3d brained/Shutterstock; 77, Mark Thiessen, NGP; 78, Dinga/Shutterstock; 79, Mark Evans/iStockphoto; 80, Bonnie Marsh/National Geographic My Shot; 81 (LOLE), H. Brauer/Shutterstock; 81

(RT), oriontrail/Shutterstock; 81 (UPLE), Jenny Solomon/Shutterstock; 82-3, Marcelo Krause/Underwater Books; 85 (LE), David Quinn; 85 (LORT), George Shiras, III/National Geographic Stock; 85 (UPRT), George Shiras, III; 86 (CTR), Brown Reference Group; 86 (LO), Wil Tirion; 86 (UPLE), thrashem/Shutterstock; 86 (UPRT), bhathaway/Shutterstock; 87 (LO), stockpix4u/Shutterstock; 87 (UP), Stubblefield Photography/Shutterstock; 88 (CTR), Tupungato/Shutterstock; 88 (LORT), Ding Ming, Zhejiang Museum of Natural History; 88 (UPLE), 3d brained/Shutterstock; 89 (LE), Igor Kali/Shutterstock; 89 (RT), Hernan Canellas/National Geographic Stock; 90, optimarc/Shutterstock; 91, Joe Petersburger/National Geographic Stock; 92, Valio Vasilev/National Geographic My Shot; 93 (LOLE), dabjola/Shutterstock; 93 (RT), Kletr/Shutterstock; 93 (UPLE), Steve Cukrov/Shutterstock; 94-5, BIEL ALINO/epa/Corbis; 97 (LE), David Quinn; 97 (LORT), David Knudsen; 97 (UPRT), Tom Lovell; 98 (CTR), Brown Reference Group; 98 (LO), Wil Tirion; 98 (UPLE), thrashem/Shutterstock; 98 (UPRT), NASA/ESA/A. Riess (STScI/JHU)/L. Macri (Texas A&M University)/Hubble Heritage Team (STScI/AURA); 99 (LE), David Doubilet/National Geographic Stock; 99 (RT), Vishnevskiy Vasily/Shutterstock; 100 (CTR), Patrick Poendl/Shutterstock; 100 (LO), Shizuka Aoki/National Geographic Stock; 100 (UP), 3d brained/Shutterstock; 101, Zach Holmes/Alamy; 102, Ira Block/National Geographic Stock; 103, Joe McNally/National Geographic Stock; 104, Maxim Shatrov/National Geographic My Shot; 105 (LOLE), Vitaly Raduntsev/Shutterstock; 105 (RT), Natchapon L./Shutterstock; 105 (UPLE), Maksymilian Skolik/Shutterstock; 106-7, Scott Woodward; 109 (LE), David Quinn; 109 (LORT), Kjell Brynildsen/iStockphoto; 109 (UPRT), Howell Walker/National Geographic Stock; 110 (CTR), Brown Reference Group; 110 (LO), Wil Tirion; 110 (UPLE), thrashem/Shutterstock; 110 (UPRT), Clay Perry/Corbis; 111 (LO), BlueOrange Studio/Shutterstock; 111 (UP), Joseph Brown; 112 (LO), Vaidas Bucys/Shutterstock; 112 (UPLE), 3d brained/Shutterstock; 112 (UPRT), tororo reaction/Shutterstock; 113, kavram/Shutterstock; 114, Chepko Danil Vitalevich/Shutterstock; 115 (UP), gillmar/Shutterstock; 115 (LO), John Tomanio/National Geographic Stock; 116, Nancy Law/National Geographic My Shot; 117 (LOLE), Laurent Renault/iStockphoto; 117 (RT), Konstantin Mironov/Shutterstock; 117 (UPLE), Bob Ainsworth/Shutterstock; 118-9, Frans Lanting/National Geographic Stock; 121 (LE), David Quinn; 121 (LORT), Robin Siegel, NGS; 121 (UPRT), NASA/JSC; 122 (CTR), Brown Reference Group; 122 (LO), Wil Tirion; 122 (UPLE), thrashem/Shutterstock; 122 (UPRT), National Geographic Art; 123 (LE), JAY TOWN/AFP/Getty Images; 123 (RT), 4634093993/Shutterstock; 124 (CTR), Andrey Armyagov/Shutterstock; 124 (LOCTR, LOLE, LORT), Graphics: Lawson Parker, NGM Staff/Source: Nigel Raine, Royal Holloway, University of London; 124 (UPLE), 3d brained/Shutterstock; 124 (UPRT), Sivakumar Sathiamoorthy/iStockphoto; 125, AFP/The Institute of Cell Biophysics of the Russian Academy of Sciences/Getty Images; 126, Stefan Fichtel/National Geographic Stock; 127 (LE), Robert Clark; 127 (RT), Jason Lee/National Geographic Stock; 128, Angga Putra/National Geographic My Shot; 129 (LOLE), James Steidl/Shutterstock; 129 (RT), Artbox/Shutterstock; 129 (UPLE), Marc Dietrich/Shutterstock; 130-1, Mike Theiss/National Geographic Stock; 133 (LE), David Quinn; 133 (LORT), James L. Stanfield; 133 (UPRT), Albert Moldvay; 134 (CTR), Brown Reference Group; 134 (LO), Wil Tirion; 134 (UPLE), thrashem/Shutterstock; 134 (UPRT), Navy Medical Center San Diego; 135 (LE), Courtesy David Stephens, National Geographic Expeditions; 135 (RT), Perutskyi Petro/Shutterstock; 136 (CTR), Galyna Andrushko/Shutterstock; 136 (LO), Don Farrall/Getty Images; 136 (UP), 3d brained/Shutterstock; 137, Mark Thiessen, NGP; 138, Gregory M. Erickson; 139, Gerrit_de_Vries/Shutterstock; 140, Anurag Kumar/National Geographic My Shot; 141 (LOLE), Dudarev Mikhail/Shutterstock; 141 (RT), Todd Shoemake/Shutterstock; 141 (UPLE), STILLFX/Shutterstock; 142-3, Ralph Lee Hopkins/National Geographic Stock; 145 (LE), David Quinn; 145 (LORT), Bruce Dale; 145 (UPRT), Emory Kristof; 146 (CTR), Brown Reference Group; 146 (LO), Wil Tirion; 146 (UPLE), thrashem/Shutterstock; 146 (UPRT), Anup Shah/naturepl.com; 147 (LE), 26ISO/iStockphoto; 147 (RT), SuperStock/Getty Images; 148 (CTR), oversnap/iStockphoto; 148 (LOLE), Rebecca Hale, NGP; 148 (LORT A and B), Joe McKendry/National Geographic Stock; 148 (UP), 3d brained/Shutterstock; 149, mpanch/Shutterstock; 150, schankz/Shutterstock; 151, Maxim Tupikov/Shutterstock; 152, James Snyder/National Geographic My Shot; 153 (LOLE), Igor Klimov/Shutterstock; 153 (RT), Repina Valeriya/Shutterstock; 153 (UPLE), J. Helgason/Shutterstock.

The Best of National Geographic
Yearbook 2013

Published by the National Geographic Society

John M. Fahey, Jr., *Chairman of the Board and Chief Executive Officer*
Timothy T. Kelly, *President*
Declan Moore, *Executive Vice President; President, Publishing and Digital Media*
Melina Gerosa Bellows, *Executive Vice President; Chief Creative Officer, Books, Kids, and Family*

Prepared by the Book Division

Hector Sierra, *Senior Vice President and General Manager*
Anne Alexander, *Senior Vice President and Editorial Director*
Jonathan Halling, *Design Director, Books and Children's Publishing*
Marianne R. Koszorus, *Design Director, Books*
Amy Briggs, *Senior Editor*
R. Gary Colbert, *Production Director*
Jennifer A. Thornton, *Director of Managing Editorial*
Susan S. Blair, *Director of Photography*
Meredith C. Wilcox, *Director, Administration and Rights Clearance*

Staff for This Book

Bridget A. English, *Editor*
Heidi Egloff, *Project Editor*
Melissa Farris, *Art Director*
Sherry L. Brukbacher, *Illustrations Editor*
Linda Makarov, *Designer*
Carl Mehler, *Director of Maps*
Liz Marvin, *Picture Legends Writer*
Judith Klein, *Production Editor*
Galen Young, *Rights Clearance Specialist*
Katie Olsen, *Design Assistant*
Dee Wong, *Editorial Assistant*

Manufacturing and Quality Management

Phillip L. Schlosser, *Senior Vice President*
Chris Brown, *Vice President, NG Book Manufacturing*
George Bounelis, *Vice President, Production Services*
Nicole Elliott, *Manager*
Rachel Faulise, *Manager*
Robert L. Barr, *Manager*

The National Geographic Society is one of the world's largest non-profit scientific and educational organizations. Founded in 1888 to "increase and diffuse geographic knowledge," the Society works to inspire people to care about the planet. National Geographic reflects the world through its magazines, television programs, films, music and radio, books, DVDs, maps, exhibitions, live events, school publishing programs, interactive media and merchandise. *National Geographic* magazine, the Society's official journal, published in English and 33 local-language editions, is read by more than 40 million people each month. The National Geographic Channel reaches 370 million households in 34 languages in 168 countries. National Geographic Digital Media receives more than 15 million visitors a month. National Geographic has funded more than 10,000 scientific research, conservation and exploration projects and supports an education program promoting geography literacy. For more information, visit www.nationalgeographic.com.

For more information, please call 1-800-NGS LINE (647-5463) or write to the following address:

National Geographic Society
1145 17th Street N.W.
Washington, D.C. 20036-4688 U.S.A.

For rights or permissions inquiries, please contact National Geographic Books Subsidiary Rights: ngbookrights@ngs.org

Published 2012.
Pedigree Books Limited, Beech Hill House, Walnut Gardens, Exeter, Devon EX4 4DH
www.pedigreebooks.com | books@pedigreegroup.co.uk
The Pedigree trademark, email and website addresses, are the sole and exclusive properties of Pedigree Group Limited, used under licence in this publication.

12/PED/1